What

UnTherapy

"Sunny Massad has provided the distillation we have all been waiting for. *UnTherapy* is a smart little book, directed and utterly relevant for those of us with over-busy lives. She offers us clear choices for living fully, with grace and resilience."

Laura Sewall, Ph.D., Author
Sight & Sensibility: The Ecopsychology of Perception

"Dr. Sunny Massad provides readers with a psychological and wellness-based owner's manual."

B. Eliot Cole, MD, MPA
Executive Director, American Society of Pain Educators

"If you are on a spiritual quest or want to remember your indomitable innate qualities, then you must read *UnTherapy*! You will feel lighter, clearer, and happier."

Lama Wangchuck

"*UnTherapy* is a 'must read' that will shift your perspective and transform the way you interact with yourself and the world around you."

Dr. Laurie Steelsmith
author of *Natural Choices for Women's Health*

"This wisdom-packed book helps reframe struggles of the heart while providing eminently practical ways to break free from negative thoughts. I recommend it to all who are seeking a life that is meaningful and free."

Anita Johnston, Ph.D.
author of *Eating in the Light of the Moon*

"I love good self-help books that give practical advice and tell me something new. *UnTherapy* pulls out the plug on a lot of old stories. Read this book and help yourself to heal."

Alice Anne Parker
author of *Understand Your Dreams*
and *The Last of the Dream People*

"Dr. Massad's positive and optimistic approach helps you explore the peace of mind that comes by paradoxically accepting your negativity and pessimism --and with a genuine sense of humor, as well!"

Ragini Elizabeth Michaels
author of *How to Live with Paradox*

"We are all neurotic in one way or another. It's just part of the human condition. *UnTherapy* teaches us to accept our neurosis with compassion, while not letting it rule our lives."

Brian Samo Ross
author of *Talking to God without Calling Long Distance*

"Sunny Massad's *UnTherapy* is a breath of fresh air that reveals the truth: you are enough, right now. If you are ready to be fulfilled, satisfied and at peace with yourself and your life, then this book is a *must read."*

Linda Giles
author of *The Big Hunger*

"*UnTherapy* is exactly what we need at this time in history. It's time to stop talking and start listening. Stop doing and start being. Stop getting and start giving. This book provides the inspiration, support, and encouragement to do just that. It is not a book to speed-read, put aside, and forget. Its short sections are to be savored, their taste to linger on our minds, seep into our consciousness, and flavor our way of life."

Makana Risser Chai
author of *Lomilomi: Sacred Touch of Aloha*

"Dr. Massad's book is true preventive medicine and a must read for patients who are prepared to see life as it truly is, free of the excess baggage we so often carry. Each chapter is a mercurial key that opens and enlightens the reader to another facet of life's self-imposed burdens on the path to joyful and calm abiding."

Ira D. Zunin, M.D., M.P.H. Medical Director
Manakai O Malama Integrative Health Care Group

UnTherapy

A Positive Psychology for Enlightened Living

Art by Patty Ward and Sunny Massad
Editing by Roshani Shay, Ph.D. and Gary Culver

Hardcover ISBN: 978-1-60145-936-7
Paperback ISBN: 978-1-60145-937-4

This publication is not to be considered a rendering of psychological services nor is it intended to be used in place of psychological treatment or diagnosis. If you have any doubts regarding the suitability of the material or exercises herein, consult with a licensed clinic al therapist to determine whether this model is appropriate for you. No expressed or implied guarantee as to the effects of the use of the recommendations can be given nor liability assumed.

Printed in the United States of America
2010

UnTherapy

A Positive Psychology for Enlightened Living

Sunny Massad, Ph.D.

Acknowledgements

I humbly acknowledge the still, small voice inside that consistently provides clarity and direction. I offer my heartfelt thanks to Roshani Shay, my dear friend, ally, and editor extraordinaire, for her infinite kindness and unconditional support, and to Gary "Surta" Culver, my heart and my home, for always being present, patient, kind and so much damned fun to be with. I am ever so appreciative to each and every one of my nurturing friends who share in the ceaseless amusement that our lives continuously provide: Patty Ward, Philip Niren Toelkes, Pratibha Eastwood, Elizabeth Grannan, Kathleen Broglio, Hildegarde Goss, Shantparv Te Kau Whatitiri, and all of the other devoted friends, clients, students and mentors who have lit my path and graced my life.

The old saying, "when the student is ready, the teacher appears" has always proven to be true in my life. I have had the pleasure of studying with a number of truly great teachers, the most influential of whom was Bhagwan Shree Rajneesh, an Indian mystic of the *Crazy Wisdom* tradition who ultimately became known simply as "Osho" before he died in 1990. I have also been deeply influenced by the teachings of William James, J. Krishnamurti, Aldous Huxley, Alan Watts, Abraham Maslow, William Glasser, Pema Chodron, Stephen Levine, Gerald Jampolsky, Ragini Michaels, Ken Wilbur, and particularly, Martin Seligman's scientific research relating to positive psychology. While the contents of this book may not represent their teachings, *per se*, each provided a vital nudge that informed this practical model for conscious living.

Contents

Foreword
by Arjuna Ardagh

Many years ago, after a long period of working hard without much of a break, I took an extended sabbatical. We rented out our house, put everything in storage and traveled to Asia for a long period of meditation and retreat. We lived like that for almost two years: no computer, no TV, no telephone. Highly recommended.

We returned to live in America after my wife got pregnant (see what trouble having no TV and computer gets you up to?). We settled back into our old lives in Seattle and I began my teaching career again. After just a few weeks, I received an invitation to conduct a series of evening events on Orcas Island, a wild, remote location reached only by ferry. My organizer kindly made her house available to me and went to stay with a friend. The house was situated on a huge property. The nearest neighbors were ten minutes' drive away. It was built on a hillside exposed to the wind and would creak and groan as the northern Pacific weather tested the foundation's stability.

One afternoon during that trip I went into town to the local video store. Because I hadn't seen a movie in a long time, I wanted to ease back into it gently, nothing too traumatic. I was in a Walt Disney mood. I looked through the titles and dismissed them one by one: too violent, too scary, too gross, too weird, too this, too that. But then I found a title that really caught my eye. It starred Anthony Hopkins, one of my long time favorite Shakespearean actors, and the title suggested peace and serenity. It even had a picture of a butterfly on the cover. This was sure to be a feel-good movie. I went to the counter with my choice for the evening: *Silence of the Lambs*.

The event ended around 10:00 PM, and I settled into the silence of my solitary abode. With nothing to do the next morning, I figured I might as well watch my feel-good movie, so I slipped it into the VCR.

It took me about 15 minutes to realize the false assumption I had made, but by then it was too late, I was hooked. As the story continued from one grim and terrifying scenario to another, the rattling caused by the trees blowing against the windows of the house became more and more ominous. If you've ever seen the movie, you know what I am talking about. As the lurid psyche of Hannibal Lector became at the same time more enticing and sinister, the creaking of that old house left me more and more nervous.

About half way through the movie I found myself in an interesting predicament, almost as though I had an on/off switch at my disposal. If I gave myself completely to the movie and allowed myself to be drawn into its carefully crafted reality, my body would enter into tremendous stress. Small rustling sounds became terrifying, terrible images of meeting a grisly end, leaving my as yet unborn son fatherless, became vivid and real. It only took a little flip of awareness to zoom out from the movie and to recognize, once again, that I am here, I am sitting on a comfortable sofa in my friend's spacious and charming old house, eating Ben and Jerry's ice-cream, with a fridge full of good food and plenty of time on my hands, on one of the most beautiful islands in the world. I have a healthy body; I have a wife and good friends and am about to be a father. All is well. Yes, there is a movie playing, with which I can choose the relationship I want.

Flipping that switch backwards and forwards throughout the evening, I realized both positions had their attractions. To be fully involved in the movie was entertaining, exciting, and an adrenaline rush. But, to be too much involved became terrifying and stressful. Detaching from the movie became cozy, familiar and safe. Detaching too much denied the point of renting it in the first place. Hovering between those two positions, involved and entertained yet uninvolved and present, I managed to make it all the way through *Silence of the Lambs* and still sleep soundly that night.

The brilliantly simple yet profound book that you hold now in your hands offers you that same kind of a switch to flip: one that can radically transform your relationship to all experience.

Most of us, most of the time, get drawn into the thoughts and reactive feelings generated by our minds, in such a way that we lose any perspective on what is truly happening. When anger comes, we don't even realize that we are angry. We only see the story of a person who has wronged us. When lust takes over our vision, we lose the perspective that we are having a hormonal response in the body, and the object of our desire becomes our fixation. When our attention is glued to thoughts and feelings in this way, we have very limited options. One knee jerk reaction is to try to change the outer world. *If only he listened more. If only she'd have sex with me more often. If only they paid me more money.* At some point, perhaps, we realize the futility of these efforts, and we "mature" into trying to change ourselves. This is the domain of conventional therapy. We try to unravel all of the things that have been done to us from the past, hoping that one day we can create an ideal and perfect psyche that allows us to finally enjoy life.

Sunny Massad belongs to an emerging, new way of working with the mind which has its roots in both the best of Western Psychology as well as a mystical perspective derived from Eastern traditions. There are some things you just can't fix if you are at the same time identified with *being* them. A brain surgeon, for example, could do great work on someone else's brain, but not on his own. If you want to make changes to the operating system of the computer you are using, you have to boot up the computer from a CD or external drive, you can't use the computer to change the same system that is running it. And ever tried tickling yourself, or telling yourself a joke, or even surprising yourself? Can't be done. In the same way, there is not a whole lot you can do to change the contents of your thinking, if you are at the same time identified with being those very thoughts and beliefs.

Perhaps the most revolutionary step that a human can make is to be able to observe their own thinking process, and to realize that who they actually are is something deeper, more mysterious, and more expansive than any thought the mind has ever created. This is called "Awakening," and it allows us not only a freedom from the constriction of the mind, like taking off a tight shoe, but also allows us for the first time to be able to make conscious and fresh choices to welcome thoughts which are useful and creative.

Sunny Massad is eminently qualified to write a book of this kind for three important reasons.

First, she has versed herself in a wide variety of traditions and can draw from the very best of practical mysticism. She is comfortable with the Buddhists and can speak their language, but she also understands the Christian mystics, the Sufis, and the Judaic tradition.

Second, Sunny has also immersed herself in the cutting edge of western psychology. She obtained her Ph.D. at Saybrook University under the direct supervision of Stanley Krippner, one of the leading authorities today on the nature of consciousness. So she is just as familiar with Freud, Jung, cognitive therapy, and even neurolinguistic programming.

But her third qualification eclipses the other two completely. Sunny Massad is a true mystic and has done her own inner work for real: both in the exploration of our eternal, expansive awakened nature, as well as our unavoidable shadow self. She has traveled into the light and also explored the darkness.

This book represents the finest in the field of "Translucent Psychology." It sits alongside the great contributions of A.H. Almaas, Jacqulyn Small and Stanlislav Grof. Her approach is not opaque: which means that she is not approaching human beings as defined by their thoughts and feelings or even their sense of personal identity. But her approach is also not aiming for total transparency and transcendence: an attempt to deny our humanity and disappear into the light. A translucent approach is one that allows us to be both human and universal simultaneously, as a paradox that could never be fully reconciled intellectually, but can only be lived as an exquisite mystery. With elegance, humor, and practical insight, Sunny brings together seemingly disparate elements which give us the tools we need to return to being simple and natural in our humanity.

Arjuna Ardagh, author of *the Translucent Revolution*
Founder of the Awakening Coaching Training

Truth is inexpressible.
It has to be discovered.

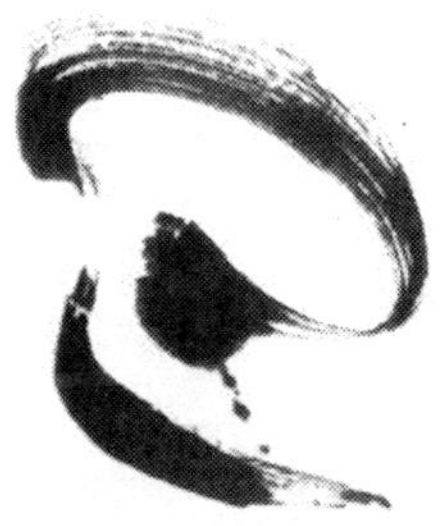

Nothing in this book should be considered
"the truth" in absolute terms.

UnTherapy is merely a useful model
for alleviating suffering.

We must be the change we wish to see in the world.
Mahatma Gandhi

Introduction
A Handbook for Conscious Living

This is a handbook for enlightened living that was designed for highly functional adults who want to live even richer lives. It is not intended to serve as a substitute for therapeutic or pharmacological intervention. Rather, my hope is that this book will support and inspire you in those moments when you feel out of balance, drained, or weary.

UnTherapy proposes that peace of mind occurs as a result of waking up to how one's own thoughts affect, and even determine one's feelings. Such awareness can stimulate a metamorphosis of destructive thoughts, feelings, and behaviors into what Buddhists refer to as "right action." Those who experience the transformative effects of how an objective awareness of one's own internal world can reduce the shadows of self-deception and illusion do not doubt its value. And those who have no experience with objective awareness are rarely convinced of its validity by rational argument.

Enlightened living begins with one essential premise: it is okay to be you, just as you are, embracing every aspect of yourself, including your own self-judgment, which, by the way, provides an impetus to grow. *UnTherapy* proposes that you set an intention about how you wish to be and how you want to live, while simultaneously accepting the conditions of your life just as they are right now. You will learn to make peace with how your life has played itself thus far. You will also learn to free yourself from anxieties that so often occur as a result of "efforting," so that you can feel personally fulfilled throughout your journey regardless of how close or distant your goals might be.

Your commitment to participate in shaping your own fate suggests that you probably already hold your life to high standards and may already have begun the journey of dismantling the thoughts, beliefs, and behaviors that sabotage your own fulfillment. Inviting the repressed shadows of the ego to emerge into the light of awareness reveals the beauty of who you actually are, which is all too often buried beneath the superficial conditioning of societal norms. Mental, spiritual and emotional clarity does not imply an absence of neurosis, but rather an astute recognition that even neurosis is a part of who you are.

UnTherapy differs from orthodox models of psychology in one essential way. The emphasis is on helping you understand *how* you are trapped in self-defeating patterns rather than helping you to understand *why*. If you have previously read self-help books, you know that reading a book, like reading a menu, simply provides options. Although you might end up knowing more intellectually, substantial change in your attitudes or behaviors cannot occur unless you consciously invite the material to seep deeply into your consciousness. Only then will you discover how profoundly the material contained herein can affect the quality of your daily life.

Because transformation requires participation, I encourage you to use the self-reflective exercises contained herein to help you delve deeper. They are designed to heighten awareness about your own internal processes so that you can adapt dimensions of mind, action, and personality that support enlightened living rather than an unconscious life that is lived on "automatic pilot." *UnTherapy* will help you gain deeper access to the inherent wisdom that dwells beneath your thinking mind so that your most cherished values will inform your every decision. Choose well.

The Author's Story

A Note from the Author

Although I rarely consider the past to be a reference point from which to perceive present life circumstances, I have included my own life story to demonstrate that the principles in this book are not only the result of academic knowledge or degrees in psychology, but are also the result of personal insights that were gained from painful but valuable life experiences.

It is my contention that if I can transcend the fallout of family dysfunction and personal adversities, then you surely can too. If you never had the opportunity to learn how to release yourself from the tyranny of your own past, or the conclusions you drew about yourself or the world as a result of that past, this book was written for you.

The greatest revolution in our generation
is the discovery that human beings,
by changing the inner attitudes of their minds,
can change the outer aspects of their lives.
William James

The Wisdom of Insecurity

When I was eleven years old, I returned home from school and watched helplessly as my mother was being put into a straight jacket, bundled into an ambulance, and taken to a state mental institution where she would reside for the longest year of my life. She had just recently learned that my father had run away to Las Vegas with his secretary. My mother had been a stay-at-home mom with three kids for thirteen years and had no job skills to fall back on. She could not cope with the anxiety of handling the financial responsibilities alone.

My father, a rather handsome and charismatic man, happened to be a gambler who often failed to pay his debts. His move to Las Vegas, my mother feared, would insure that she would rarely, if ever, receive financial support again. She suffered from so much anxiety about how she would be able to care for her three children and herself that she snapped. To add insult to injury, just two weeks after my mother was committed, my father, a three-pack-a-day cigarette smoker, collapsed from a massive heart attack. He was only 36 years old.

In the space of two weeks, I lost access to everything that was important to me: my parents, my family, my home, my friends, my school, and even my dog. My sense of childhood security had vanished. As a child who grew up watching black and white television sitcoms where the parents seemingly provided stable, loving homes, I was ashamed to be a member of a family that did not meet the standards of "normal."

My only partially-developed personal identity had already begun to dissolve. I no longer had a sense of who I was or where I belonged. I fluctuated between being scared and excited because although I didn't quite know how to go about it, I knew that I was free to reinvent myself. I felt that I had nothing left to lose. My mother's first emotional breakdown, followed by my father's physical collapse, inspired me to search out new and different ways to live my own life. I was determined to discover better coping skills for surviving life's daily stressors than my parents had.

Like all children, I sought validation. That is what children need to feel safe and secure. I was raised a Roman Catholic. My childhood prayers were focused outward, toward a God that I imagined to be like Santa Claus in the sky who knew when I was "bad or good." If I could not feel loved and therefore worthy and valued by my parents, then God would serve as my alternative surrogate. I expected that consuming the host at Holy Communion would provide me with nothing short of a mystical experience. After all, the promise of ingesting the body of Christ in the form of a wafer surely would transport me into sacred territory. But each time I swallowed a host, nothing happened; I heard no harps, saw no fireworks, had no mystical awakening, and certainly experienced no heightened sense of safety; I was simply aware of a little, round, dry disc stuck to the roof of my mouth. Each week I confessed my sins, marched back up to the altar and hoped against hope that grace would descend upon me. I wanted with all my heart to feel the presence of the Divine, but nothing happened; no floods of love; no voice of God; not even a flash of insight about how to proceed now that my parents were gone. Even at the ripe young age of seven, I suspected that a better, more free or more holy state was possible.

Although psychologists contend that such feelings of longing for "something more" are present even before a triggering event, this was my first awareness of the nagging feeling that, "There must be something wrong with me." Despite personal triumphs, like finding new friends and maintaining good grades, discontent lurked in the background of my awareness. Like a nagging parent, an internal voice forever criticized the way I looked and how I performed. I simply assumed that because my family was broken, I was broken. I believed that if my family had remained together, I would surely have remained secure and self-assured. I was unaware, at the time, that other children experienced similar feelings despite the fact that their families were still intact.

To handle feelings of inadequacy, I relied on facades, like so many vulnerable children (and adults) learn to do, to insure that no one would discover how truly afraid I actually was. Yet despite the fact that I longed for approval, I was unable to allow it in. I believed that anyone who complimented me must have had very low standards; or perhaps they simply didn't know me intimately enough to recognize my unworthiness. So I was caught in a destructive cycle: the more insecure I felt, the more self-deprecating thoughts arose. And the more self-deprecating thoughts I had, the more I caused myself to feel inadequate, and thus even more insecure.

The negative conclusions that I drew about myself and about life arose out of some very painful and even terrifying experiences. My warm, kind, but extremely fragile mother, later diagnosed with both bipolar disorder and paranoid schizophrenia, spent most of her adult life in and out of what were then called "mental hospitals." Until we were in our teens, each time she went into a manic episode, my brother, sister and I were rescued by friends or relatives.

When I was a teenager my mother's sister, my favorite aunt, a mother of four who pitched in when my mother was absent, committed suicide during one of her own particularly debilitating depressions. My grandmother, on my mother's side of the family tree, also spent years in and out of mental institutions and halfway houses. As a result, I spent much of my childhood visiting female "role models" who were locked away in wards filled with fearful, depressed, sometimes raging and out of control adults who were generally heavily sedated. I yearned to find a model of living that would help me to better cope.

Leap and the Net will appear

As soon as I turned 18 years old, I moved out of the house to find my own way in the world. Although I loved my mother dearly, I was no longer willing to or capable of fulfilling the role of child caregiver. I was hell-bent on finding healthy role models to teach me how to live. Being a descendent of a long line of "crazy" women and with an absent and irresponsible father certainly provided me with sufficient alibis to justify feelings of blame and shame. But I got tired of moving through life as a victim and set out to discover ways to develop my strengths.

As a result of feeling a low sense of self-worth, I believed that becoming healthy would require great effort on my part. This notion was based on the fundamental premise that self-improvement was not only necessary, but attainable, and would result from extraordinary efforts to perfect the inadequate parts of myself. I believed, like so many others, that personal development was a path that ascended upward, so I would inevitably evolve as the result of "working on" myself. I dedicated an inordinate amount of time, money, and energy to the pursuit of happiness.

Growing up in unconventional circumstances was partly a contributor to the fact that I was never drawn to become a part of the "American dream." Because of the history of mental illness in my family, I was not inclined to risk having children of my own. Nor did I long to have a house with a white picket fence or even a traditional career. What I yearned for was peace of mind. I spent years underlining formulas, highlighting theories, and putting stars in the margins of psychology, philosophy, and self-help books. But the knowledge that I gathered from reading did not result in a particularly quiet mind or dissolution of my inner critic. Nor did such experiences, although rewarding in many other ways, provide me with a sense of security. None of that "borrowed knowledge" resulted in any real or lasting change in my thoughts, feelings, or behavior, despite my ability to intellectually understand.

I learned how to use self-hypnosis to increase self-discipline, listened to wise teachers and radical revolutionaries, participated in group therapy, attended seminars, got into and out of challenging relationships that I justified as being "good for my growth," expanded my consciousness with mind-altering substances, attuned myself with body work, bonded with friends, moved to the country to live off the land, and traveled the world on a shoestring budget with nothing more than a pack on my back. Like so many seekers of my generation, I had always believed that if I worked hard enough on myself, took risks, sustained deep relationships, and lived amidst the beauty of nature, I would ultimately outgrow my insecurities.

While I experienced many moments of satisfaction, I also ended up with a longer and longer "to do" list. Each time I reached a milestone, like becoming financially independent, rather than pausing to acknowledge my triumph, I forged ahead to tackle the next big challenge. I never felt that I had enough and more importantly, I never felt like I was enough. Each time I reached a goal, I raised the bar just a little bit higher, so despite all that I accomplished, I continuously felt that I still had a long way to go before I could relax.

I am deeply grateful to have had the opportunity to discover fun and supportive friends, to immerse myself in loving, intimate relationships, to become a member of several wonderful communities filled with interesting and creative people, and to live in a number of exquisitely serene locations. But like all seekers, I held a high standard for myself that managed to stay just beyond my reach, despite decades of accomplishment. Although I was an optimist about external things, I was a pessimist about my ability to become free from the wounds of my past. Although I was unaware of it at the time, my desire to change and to grow, to be "fixed" and to be "free," stemmed from my inability to accept myself, or more precisely, to accept the feelings of vulnerability that resulted from the loss of a familiar structure that had once provided a sense of security, even if it had been a false one.

As a child of the 1950's, I was raised in the cultural climate that taught me to work hard and be my best. I became the victim of an idealized version of the person I believed I should and could become. I set out to become enlightened, which would render me fearless and free of all neurosis. But as long as I anticipated becoming freer, greater, higher, or more fulfilled one day in the future, present satisfaction eluded me. I was caught in the endless web of desire, hoping that I would find something, someone, or some place that would permanently save me from my sense of inadequacy. I had been, as the song goes, "looking for love in all the wrong places."

Stuck in My Story No More

I began reading books by Aldous Huxley, William James, J. Krishnamurti and Alan Watts while I was still in high school. I resonated with their recognition that a transformation of consciousness would be beneficial not only personally, but also to humanity and the world at large. Years later, I was given some books by Rajneesh, who ultimately became known as "Osho" before he died in 1990. I resonated with his call to "awaken the sleeping Buddha within" and felt compelled to meet him. I traveled to India to immerse myself in his invitation to live and work within an environment that supported meditative practice.

He identified the cultural shifts of the 1960's and 70's as a revolution of consciousness that would replace centuries of living from set beliefs with a new quest to discover one's own truth. His essential message was to drop the facades of the ego and the chatter in the mind and become innocent again so that God could be more accessible and love could return to the heart.

The seven years that I spent in his presence were, without a doubt, the most transformative years of my life. I no longer used self-reflection time to try to make dreams come true or pain go away. The silent awareness of meditation combined with the personal responsibility that arose from self-reflection, promoted a sense of well-being from which the desire for selfless service naturally evolved. I still set intentions about my future, but my attention became more focused on who I was becoming as a person.

In the 1990's, I enrolled in graduate school to sink my teeth into the emerging humanistic and transpersonal psychologies as they related to consciousness studies. Although I found it difficult to find a graduate program that focused on precisely what I wanted to study, I eventually found one that would allow me to do my Master's level research on Osho's *Psychology of the Buddhas* and my Ph.D. dissertation on the subject of ego transcendence.

I spent six long years investigating and interviewing people who reportedly had "transcendent experiences" that endured beyond just a few weeks or months. My immersion into the intimate and detailed descriptions of spiritual awakening proved to be a provocative journey. The very activity of conducting that research was an unexpected act of self-purification. The paradox of consciousness studies is that they are attempts to discover something that cannot be obtained through thought. No cognition, however ingenuous, can ever satisfactorily capture the immensely diverse scope of dimensionality that creates the human experience.

At a certain point in my own evolution, my personal identification as "a seeker" became an obstacle. My yearning to "find" deterred me from fully appreciating the grace of the present. As soon as I dropped the search, I was able to relax more deeply into the ever present love that resides within and all around the living breathing organism I refer to as "me."

UnTherapy is based on the hypothesis that living consciously is, by its very nature, transformative. The objective is to integrate the drive for spiritual awakening with a larger understanding of human nature, human development, and human behavior.

If you happen to be particularly ambitious, I celebrate your accomplishments and honor the creative drive that has undoubtedly brought you success throughout your lifetime. I also hope that this book will serve to reverse the fallout of self-neglect that can sometimes result from the drive to be, to do and to have more. *UnTherapy* celebrates the resilience of the human spirit and brings into consciousness the importance of remembering that the journey of life itself is the objective.

Chapter 1
Resilience of the Human Spirit

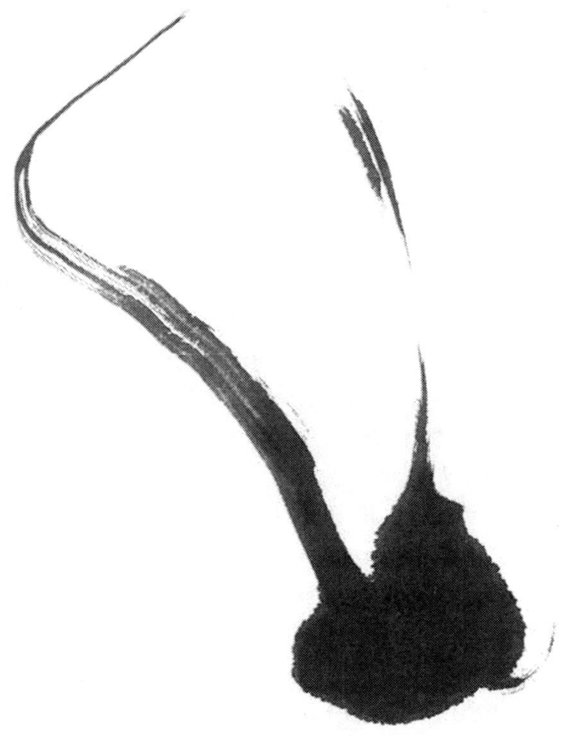

You cannot fix yourself because you are not broken.
The more you try to fix, the more you find to fix.
Only wholeness heals.
Alan Cohen

UnTherapy

As a synthesis of Asian philosophies and Western psychologies, *UnTherapy* proposes that a more objective awareness exists than the normal waking conscious state and that this objective awareness, by its very nature, is the source of character and virtue. The transformation of a person's behavior, then, is dependent upon clarity; that clarity that arises from self-reflection, from silence, and from objective awareness of one's own unconscious patterns. Such clarity allows the boundaries of "self" to expand to include the unity of all things, thereby restoring a sense of primal security and well-being, which is your natural state. The means for accessing it are within your grasp.

Western psychology has adopted a linear concept of life in which improvement and progress are perceived as end goals. A visual representation might look something like this:

Past	Present	Golden Future
Mistakes	Not quite Good Enough	Finally Free

But in the East, the wheel of life is a symbol of circular motion. Change occurs on the wheel like seasons change from year to year. Although people have their preferences, winter is not in actuality better than or an improvement upon summer. Each season of life brings aspects that contribute to the perfect balance and harmony of nature. There is no question of improvement or progress. In the same way that fruit or leaves might fall from a tree in the autumn, providing nourishment for the roots of that tree, so, too, do the experiences of each season of one's life provide lessons that, when learned, inspire growth.

Western psychology has, until recently, predominantly focused on the contents of the mind. The emerging branches of humanistic and transpersonal psychologies have begun to return psychology to the original meaning of the word, which translates as a "study of the soul." Westerners often perceive "peace of mind" to be an oxymoron, having rarely, if ever experienced moments devoid of inner conflict. *UnTherapy* is an inclusive model that combines the latest discoveries of consciousness studies with the most recent findings relating to cognitive psychology. The distinction from traditional models is that it calls for a shift in perception rather than an attempt to directly adjust beliefs and behaviors. I believe that a prudent combination of clarity, intention, curiosity, humor, and self-care will naturally result in initiative and creativity.

Transpersonal psychologists contend that an individual must develop a healthy and strong ego before successfully attaining to heightened states of awareness. Osho suggested that the first thirty five years or so of life should be devoted to strengthening the ego and then, once a strong sense of identification with the "self" is felt, attention can be transferred to the expansion of awareness that lies beyond the mortal experience of "me."

The traditional view of therapy as building up the ego simply does not do justice to what people's needs actually are. Most of us have developed our egos enough; what we suffer from is the accumulated tension of that development.

Mark Epstein, M.D.

The Therapeutic Relationship

According to the National Institute of Mental Health, an estimated 26.2 percent of Americans ages 18 and older—about one in four adults—suffer from a diagnosable mental disorder in any given year. In fact, you may unknowingly be classed among the 48 million Americans who are considered by the American Psychiatric Association to be mentally ill. This does not mean that one in four adults actually has what you or I might consider a mental disorder. It simply means that the one in four Americans who turn to therapists for help in coping with life's challenges end up with a label that implies that they have a mental disorder.

Because health insurance often covers the majority of mental health costs, more and more people seek out counselors to serve as mentors and confidants. Others are seeking spiritual guides who can help them delve into existential issues relating to life's meaning and purpose. But most people do not realize that in order for their insurance to cover the cost of treatment, their counselor must designate a diagnosis in accordance with the Diagnostic and Statistical Manual of Mental Disorders (DSM) to justify their visit.

The ever-expanding number of disorder categories in the DSM pathologizes what some people might consider normal experiences, like existential anxieties, for example, which are labeled as "Anxiety Disorder," shyness, diagnosed as "Social Phobia," or lasting grief, which bears the diagnostic label of "Complicated Grief Reaction." Even a strong-willed or high-spirited child is prone to be diagnosed with "Oppositional Disorder." Fortunately, there are branches of psychology that embrace a more holistic and less pathological approach to wellness, but if the practitioners want to bill your insurance company for their services, they, too, have to commit you to a diagnosis.

Psychologists and psychiatrists alike are educated to help their patients develop personality strength in areas of their lives that are otherwise underdeveloped or compromised, sometimes as the result of a traumatic experience. Clinical psychologists are trained to assist such people to build stronger, healthier, better-functioning egos so as to become more adaptive and thus, more productive members of society.

Many people are unaware that until recently, psychiatrists, who, unlike psychologists, are able to dispense medication to their patients, receive very little counseling training. Because their education is focused on pharmacological intervention, this can often mean that when a person books an appointment to see a psychiatrist, they will more often than not leave with a prescription for a medication that will help to relieve their symptoms. Many patients, however, are unaware that the reason why they are prescribed medication is because that is what psychiatrists are trained to do. Likewise, if you go to see a surgeon about a knee injury, the surgeon will assess your knee according to whether or not she believes that surgery would remedy your problem. She would not necessarily consider other methods of treatment that are not within the parameters of her expertise.

While there is a movement within the mental health field toward a more holistic approach, the present system is laden with specialists who are trained to diagnose and treat from their specific paradigm. Nevertheless, it is the system that most people contend with so as to get the most out of their high insurance premiums. This is not to say that psychiatrists and clinical psychologists do not do a great service for the populations they are trained to serve. The advancements made in regards to psychiatric and psychoactive medications over the past fifty years have exponentially improved the quality of life of millions of people.

But people seeking help with the ordinary challenges of life, and especially those who consider themselves to be on a spiritual path, may find that "getting in touch with feelings," "rehashing the stories of the past," or taking medication to treat symptoms can be more of a hindrance than a help. In fact, the types of people who seek out my services are generally not suited to the standard therapeutic approaches available to them through their health insurance companies. Many are looking for a more direct approach that will resolve the root issues of their present dissatisfactions. Others report failing to notice substantial changes in the way they feel about themselves or the manner in which they interact with the world around them despite years of therapy.

If you choose to work with a coach or a counselor as a way to move yourself out of a life of mediocrity, consider finding one who will help you to investigate the causal connections of your experience rather than merely focusing on symptoms. It is all too common to diagnose and treat a patient with clinical depression. There is a standard protocol that generally includes pharmaceutical intervention. But nontraditional counselors will, before referring you to a licensed practitioner if, indeed, you are clinically depressed, work with you in a very different way. They were not trained to work within the model of pathology that tends to look at symptoms as they relate to diagnosable conditions. So if you are a healthy, well-functioning person who enjoys a periodic "tune up" and you feel worse when you leave your therapist's office than you did when you arrived, consider finding a counselor or coach who works outside of the DSM model of mental health. A wellness-oriented counselor might be better equipped to serve seekers and other such individuals who do not require, and, indeed might even feel impaired by, the more traditional therapeutic interventions.

What we call 'normal' is really a psychopathology of the average, so undramatic and so widely spread that we don't even notice it.

Abraham Maslow

Options for Change

Western psychological culture adheres to the notion that painful early life experiences can result in damaging emotional aftereffects, sometimes for the rest of one's life. While this can certainly be true in cases of severe psychological trauma, the concept of "woundism" has indoctrinated the greater culture and resulted in a society that is quick to blame. Yet studies show that people who were deeply hurt as children are capable of tremendous resilience. Once they learn how to reframe the pain of their past, they generally flow more easily with change, often possess excellent crisis management skills, and tend to work well under pressure.

There is a point at which telling one's story can be therapeutic: during the period of grief that follows a death, for example. In other, more normal circumstances, however, repeating a story again and again can keep an otherwise healthy person continuously identified with the drama that is connected to that story. The more the story gets told, whether in a therapeutic or social situation, the more it is kept alive. Chronic grief about one's life story can even degenerate into self-pity, so dwelling on tales of personal tragedy past the necessary amount of time it takes to process an event can result in re-injury over and over again.

If you are a human being, you will experience pain no matter who your parents were or how your siblings, teachers, or peers may have behaved towards you. And unless there were exceptionally traumatic experiences that caused you deep, irreversible anguish, analyzing your past will not necessarily help you to feel better. In fact, dredging up painful memories may actually perpetuate your inability to enjoy the present. When you stop dividing life into good and bad, right and wrong, sick and healthy, life is just life, with seasons and cycles, like changes in the weather.

When therapy feels more like whining than anything else, when you recognize that painful experiences have provided profound lessons and insights that you might not have had without them, and when you outgrow the defenses you developed as survival strategies to cope with your childhood, the pains of the past will effortlessly fall away in the same way that ripe fruit falls from a tree. Once you come to realize that your negative attitudes and resentments no longer serve you, advance to the "Yes, it sucked, and I'm ready to move on" phase. This is the point at which it is important to seek out a counselor who is solution-oriented rather than a therapist who begins with some version of the question "What seems to be the problem?" Negative questions generate negative answers which inevitably will lead you right back into identification with your saga. Once you are no longer identified with your own history, it is then that you might become inclined to lend a hand to others who suffer in ways that you once did.

Those things that hurt, instruct.
Benjamin Franklin

Wounds

You do not, in actuality, have to remain feeling broken or irreversibly damaged by the heartbreaking events of your past. You are human and human beings are built to survive. *UnTherapy* recognizes and celebrates the resilience of the human spirit. That is not to say that repressed or unresolved issues or feelings relating to devastating experiences cannot prolong one's mental anguish or cause the heart to shut down. But carrying stories of guilt, shame or blame into the present only serves to keep that past alive.

Many people do, indeed, feel scarred by old wounds, partly because our culture supports the idea of "woundism" and partly because most people don't know how to release themselves from the grief of their own life history. *UnTherapy* imparts an opportunity to resolve feelings about the past so that you can step more fully into the present, secure in the knowledge that you have survived.

Regardless of how deeply you may have been hurt, those scars from the past can not only heal, they can serve as essential markers to arouse you to move forward; out of the shadow and into the light. There may no longer be any trace of the physical scars that marked the triumph of learning to ride your first bicycle. Each spill taught you what not to do the next time you got back up on that bike. The same principle applies to emotional scarring. When the lessons of painful experiences are recognized, hurt and resentments will begin to lift.

There are two educations.
One should teach us how to make a living
and the other how to live.
John Adams

Vulnerability

At your birth, when the umbilical cord was cut and you began to breathe on your own, you most likely cried for the first time. Regardless of how soft the blankets might have been, how dim the lights, or how warm the room, compared to the first nine months of floating in warm amniotic fluid, comforted by your mother's ever-present heartbeat and the safety and comfort of her womb, the birth experience must have been a frightening first adventure. Perceiving the sights, smells, tastes, and sounds of a foreign world resulted in a sense of being separate, dependent and vulnerable. If someone had not taken care of you at that time, you would not have survived. Of all the mammals, human beings are the most immature at birth and require the longest period of development before becoming self-sufficient.

Fear of not surviving is an appropriate response to the helplessness experienced during those first years of life. That fear arose from the fragile, finite, temporary nature of living in a separate mortal body that was utterly dependent upon the care of others. Such vulnerability causes children to look to the external to get their basic needs for safety and comfort met. It is also true that how you presently cope with existential issues like fear and loneliness continue to shape the course of your life.

Imagine how different your life would be today if you had been taught how to calm your mind when worried, how to cope with emotional pain, how to communicate when you feel threatened, and even how to fall asleep at night when your mind won't quiet down. As these skills are generally not taught by parents, teachers or clergy, it is no wonder that both children and adults suffer from feelings of inadequacy about how to cope with life's most basic stressors.

In more primitive cultures it is customary to initiate adolescents into adulthood with a rite of passage. Such rituals stimulate young people to recognize that they have internal resources that they have spent a lifetime developing and can continue to draw upon. They no longer need to depend on others for their emotional survival. This insight produces confidence and trust in one's own ability to endure. Young adults can then enjoy a give-and-take relationship with friends, family, and lovers instead of feeling scared and needy. But children raised in Western cultures do not generally have such a ritual. As a result, many young adults look to others to provide them with a sense of safety and comfort. How could they do otherwise? If they were not taught how to be physically or emotionally self-sufficient, or, if they did not have access to healthy role models, they simply may not have ever learned how to tap into their own sense of well-being.

What is necessary to change a person
is to change his awareness of himself.
Abraham Maslow

Self-Image

As a vulnerable infant, with physical and emotional needs that could only be met by someone else, a separate sense of self was bound to develop. Although you were most likely aware that you were a part of a family, a community, and perhaps even the natural order of the world around you, unconsciously the primordial fears of being separate, alone, and vulnerable could not help but to inform your outlook on life.

As the ego develops, small children generally lose awareness of the vast reality beyond their subjective sense of self and begin to believe that their individual ego is a distinct entity, separate from others and from the environment. This is how the first feelings of alienation arise. When you were afraid and alone, you had to rely on the generosity of others to meet your every need. The "separate self," or ego, is merely a reflection of how your caregivers treated you. If you were neglected or abused, the perception that you were unlovable most likely became a part of your self-concept. If you were treated with love and care, the feeling of being valued may have more positively shaped your self-image.

As you grew older, you had no choice but to act in accordance with the self-image that reflected the thoughts, feelings, and behaviors of each important person with whom you interacted. And now, as an adult, you are probably subjected to a constant stream of judgments, ideas, criticisms, plans, regrets, and opinions of your own. Of the apparently 80,000 thoughts that psychologists say the mind generates in a day, many are endlessly repetitive.

Buddhists have another perspective. They have contended for over five thousand years that there is no actual mind and therefore the ego is simply a mental construct that is not much more than a succession of thoughts. The ego, from this perspective, is a verb. Whenever you identify with thought, or, more precisely, whenever you believe that you *are* your thoughts, and that the content of your thoughts is absolute, and therefore true, that identification with your mind can cause you to perceive your "self" as a separate entity, unrelated to the rest of creation.

Liberation from the ego's perception of being separate requires access to a broader awareness that includes a separate sense of self that is part of the larger whole. The Tibetans refer to this larger whole as *rigpa:* a primordial intelligence, perpetually radiant and awake, that permeates all living things.

Just trust yourself,
then you will know how to live.
Goethe

Conditioning

An aspect unique to Western culture is that almost all experiences are understood through the rational mind and its layers of accumulated knowledge. Whether this preoccupation with the rational mind is the upshot of the seductive rewards of science and technology or the fear that a contemplative life may prove to be an unproductive one, is open to speculation. But there is no question that the predominant identification with the mind is related to a general uneasiness, dissatisfaction and even despair about the physical and emotional aspects of the "self."

The root of your dissatisfactions is not to be found in problems themselves, but rather in the way that you think about them.

UnTherapy explores dimensions of mind, action, and personality that go beyond, and transcend the general concepts of ego and personal identity common to Western theories of personality adjustment. The fundamental premise is that life is a process of discovery. Rather than focusing on perfecting aspects of the "self" that are less than virtuous, awareness opens to "waking up" from unconscious patterns that cause suffering.

Deprogramming unwanted beliefs and behaviors requires incredible awareness, but becoming conscious of the thinking/feeling mechanism helps create distance from an outdated or undesirable self-image. How deeply has your early life conditioning influenced the way you react to the world around you? Habitual programming that is rooted in an unexamined past can sabotage clarity and thus prevent appropriate responses to present situations.

Most people are totally unaware that they are the creators of their life experience. They don't see the connection between perception and experience. But the root of a person's suffering is not so much found in difficult people or circumstances as in the meaning that is attributed to those people or circumstances. In the absence of subjective opinion, life is neutral; it is simply the way it is.

How rarely are we able to let anyone see us as we are, without donning a mask of some kind.

John Welwood

Ego

The egoic mind has its own agenda: it wants to appear "okay." But the ego is a fear-based mechanism. It is always uncertain and, therefore, often conflicted. Although our culture generally considers fear to be a sign of weakness, unrecognized and unaccepted fear is at the root of most "negative" feelings. Many people attempt to hide their fears because of a belief that being afraid implies cowardice. And when insecurity, the basis of low self-esteem, is expressed as self-doubt, the ego may practice self-deception by attempts to hide feelings of inadequacy.

This unawareness, or denial of fear, can result in a spiral of escapism. Most distressing of all, the layer of protection built to shelter a person from the fear of getting hurt can even prevent love from entering a life. But fear itself is not what causes problems. Rather, it is the unawareness of fear that does so.

Listen carefully to how others speak and you will become aware of how they scare themselves. "What if the plane goes down? What if I can't earn enough money to keep up with my debts? What if I'm depressed for the rest of my life?" Such questions can sabotage your own trust and confidence. The only way out is to train the mind to take refuge in the present.

Self-Reflection

Identify a few of your own most common "What ifs?"
Example: What if I lose my source of income?

Now reassure yourself with facts about the present.
Right now, there IS no problem except my own indulgence in worrying. If it happens, I can handle it. I always land on my feet.

The more you try to fix, the more you find to fix.
Only wholeness heals.
Alan Cohen

Judgment

What people generally assume to be reality is actually only their interpretation of it. Cognitive biases continuously shape our selective attention, perceptions, and interpretation of past and present experiences. Perceived opposites are actually unifying complementaries that create a balanced whole. Unfortunately, the mind divides life into "good" and "bad." It is good to be happy and bad to be sad, or even worse, to be angry. It is good to be healthy but bad to be sick. It is good to be alive but "bad" to be dead. Each of us has a different list of preferences. Some common ones might include a list that looks something like this:

GOOD	**BAD**
wealth and abundance	poverty and debt
strength	weakness
love	fear
peace	conflict
health	sickness
happiness	sadness
comfort	discomfort
life	death

To have preferences is to be human. There is no problem there. But when experiences perceived as undesirable are resisted or pushed away, stress may arise because life often presents experiences that do not fit into a desired agenda about how life "should" be.

As much as you might prefer health, vitality, and peace you will nonetheless at some point be subjected to illness, exhaustion, and inevitable moments of conflict. It is perfectly reasonable to prefer life over death, wealth over poverty, success over failure, heaven over hell, health over sickness, and youth over aging. Obviously, if you hold life-affirming values, you will probably not be drawn toward the idea of dying any time soon. But the perception that there is something wrong when aging begins to deteriorate the body or mind, or when times of sickness or scarcity arise, is the source of much psychological suffering.

Criticism and judgment often stem from feelings of insecurity. When you begin to accept your own weaknesses and mistakes, you will find it much easier to accept the "flaws" in others. Watch the next time you feel judgmental about someone. How much of that judgment is driven by a desire to feel better about yourself?

Although resistance will keep you in a state of tension and anxiety, accepting "what is," does not necessarily mean that you should not aspire to create a comfortable future, or that you should lie down and play dead when life hands you unwanted circumstances! In fact, only when you embrace the paradoxes of reality can you effectively respond to them. Suffering ensues when the mind's view of existence is polarized to such an extent that the inherent contradictions of life become unacceptable. Liberation occurs when clear perception informs one's view of reality without biases, preferences, and other distortions.

So in what circumstances might it be inappropriate, dangerous or unethical to accept "what is?" Obviously, it would be unconscionable to take a passive stance when basic human needs, whether your own or someone else's, are unmet or violated. Standing up for what is right indicates a deep reverence and respect for life. If your judgment is based on objective perception, then allow it to serve as your conscience, directing your energy to find and implement solutions.

Liberation does not result from being free of the "negatives" of life. Liberation occurs as a consequence of being free from the perception that half of existence is positive and half is negative, half is "good" and half is "bad." Imagine how different the world would be if death were universally accepted as an inevitable and natural culmination of life, pain as a necessary communication from the body, and sadness as a necessary emotion of the heart.

Choosing acceptance over resistance is a profoundly liberating formula that promotes a drama-free life. Regardless of the ups and downs of life, peace occurs when you stop exclusively operating from projected ideals about how you and others and life itself "should" be. A deep serenity emerges when you learn to say "yes" to the moment. Some people habitually "awfulize" or indulge in negative thoughts about situations that are outside of their control. But you have the freedom and power to determine how to think about each event and how you think about it has a direct effect on how you feel and behave.

Getting a flat tire is always an abrupt and unexpected interruption. But the way in which you think about remedying the situation affects whether or not you prolong the painful event into a full day of suffering. If you tell yourself, "This is a drag, it's going to be such a hassle to deal with, why does this always have to happen to me?," you are bound to psych yourself into a tizzy. If you appease yourself with sensible thoughts like, "Tires go flat sometimes. I'll just roll with it and get on with the day," odds are that the flat tire event will feel like nothing more than a nuisance.

Needing approval is tantamount to saying, 'Your view of me is more important than my own opinion of myself.'
Wayne Dyer

Acceptance

An important part of accepting reality *just as it is* requires accepting yourself *just as you are.* Self-Acceptance does not imply a lowering of standards. On the contrary, acceptance in this context requires taking responsibility for how you may have participated in putting yourself in the creation of your present circumstances.

Putting effort into fixing or adjusting parts of yourself that you do not like may seem like a reasonable way to accelerate your own evolution. But such efforts are based on the fundamental premise that self-improvement is necessary, and that it takes "work" to transform. Both struggle and indulgence crystallize the egoic identity. In fact, many people create and perpetuate problems to escape feelings of emptiness and substantiate a strong sense of self. The ego thrives on judgment because that allows it to feel separate. Judgments then create feelings of stress, fear, and hostility, and round and round it goes. If you are tired of struggle and the drama that comes along with it, notice how much you resist and say "no" to the present. That part that wants to control, that defends its conviction to always be right, (which it very well may be, by the way), creates a tension between what you want and what is.

The desire to be "fixed, "free," or even "enlightened" stems from the belief that where you are right now is not good enough. While it is perfectly natural and healthy to have a longing to improve, incessantly chasing after desires can rob you of the opportunity to be at peace in the here and now. Granted, it is not always easy to strike a healthy balance between an aspiration to evolve and an unconditional acceptance of yourself and your life as it is. But incessant tail-chasing can cause the ego to begin to exclusively focus on its inadequacies.

It is perfectly healthy to look forward to a positive future. But dependence on the future, without acceptance of one's present state, can cause happiness and satisfaction to elude you. Unless you are deeply grounded in the present, endless pursuits may have a tendency to distract you from appreciating the precise point of the journey that you are on right now.

An essential function of the mind is obviously to solve problems. Consequently, if you don't have a problem, the mind will tend to create one. Remember when you were a kid and a sibling or bully teased you? As long as he got a reaction, he continued to badger relentlessly. Awareness of the futility and artificiality of the mind's proclivity to continuously generate problems can ultimately produce a desire to stop engaging with them. Once you do, you will accept yourself as you actually are rather than judging yourself for not yet being the way you wish that you were. Ironically, once you accept yourself as you actually are, a metamorphosis begins.

If you want an orchid to bloom, you nourish and nurture it. As you give it what it needs, it begins to blossom. The "improvement" naturally occurs as a result of creating the proper conditions in which it can thrive. Likewise, self-acceptance is the preliminary condition in which human beings begin to blossom. Once you accept your present condition, you can identify what needs to happen to create even better circumstances in which you can flourish. If an orchid has aphids, you don't spend a lot of time figuring out how they got there. You accept the plight and adjust the conditions in such a way that the aphids will no longer thrive on the orchid.

Chapter 2
The Challenges of Being Human

Moving on is a gift you give yourself.
Joan Rivers

Childhood

There are as many people who thrive despite their challenging pasts, indeed, maybe even because of their pasts, as there are people who feel victimized by them. The ability to survive insurmountable obstacles is a living testament to the fortitude of the spirit. While it can certainly be difficult to maintain faith when your world is falling apart or to love yourself when it seems like no one else does, life does not have to feel like a constant struggle. There are other, more graceful ways to move through life than simply bouncing from one drama to the next.

Your personal life story, including memories of all the injustices you have experienced over the course of your life, helps to shape your personal identity. You have the ability to dwell on the pain and injustices or to remember your life story with an empathetic heart. If your father was an alcoholic who beat you, you can choose to remember how it felt to be victimized by him. You can focus on how pathetic he was. Or you can allow yourself to gain access to a broader vision that includes not only your experience, but his as well. When you can allow yourself to realize how wounded he must have been to have inflicted such pain on his own child, the memory of his abuse will have less hold on you. There is no doubt that making your peace with people who have betrayed your trust can be difficult. And of course no one wants to condone abusive behavior. But one does not make the choice to re-evaluate horrendous situations with an empathetic heart out of a sense of denial or even out of a sense of generosity. One makes the choice to embrace empathy because releasing anger and resentment is a transformational act that emancipates the spirit. To hold on to one's judgments perpetuates and prolongs suffering. Although you will never be able to create a different past, your past does not necessarily have to determine your present. You can change your point of view so that memories have less power over your present emotions and actions. You are at liberty to rewrite the script of your life from a new vantage point.

Self-Reflection

In what way are you still feeling resentful toward people who once hurt you?
Example: I still resent receiving an I.O.U for Christmas and then, after months of waiting, never ending up with a gift from my father.

What is a larger perspective that can release you from the toxic effects of that memory?
Example: Considering he had just survived a massive heart attack and the disintegration of his marriage, his financial and emotional burdens may have blinded him to recognizing how important Christmas is to a child.

It is what a man thinks of himself that really determines... his fate.

Henry David Thoreau

Fear

Events such as divorce, the loss of a job, a frightening diagnosis, or a brush with death, can threaten one's sense of security, but also inspire the realization that security, like joy, cannot be permanently attained. However, the ego feels threatened by situations that are beyond its control. So death, rejection, and abandonment result in feelings of powerlessness.

> Until self-acceptance, self-compassion, and self-encouragement are learned, insecurities may continue to lurk just beneath the surface of awareness.

Because of those early life dependencies on "other," children cannot help but look outside of themselves to get their needs for safety and comfort met. But most adults create unconscious internal strategies to placate uncomfortable feelings related to existential angst. Attempts to get one's most basic needs for safety and comfort met by friends, family members, or even the accumulation of status, possessions, or net worth often work for periods of time, but ultimately fail. Authentic happiness requires one to focus on having a rich inner life as well.

Everyone needs to discover how to validate and care for themselves, especially as a prelude to enjoying healthy, adult relationships. Until self-acceptance, self-compassion, and self-encouragement are learned, insecurities may continue to lurk just beneath the surface of awareness. When you manage to have a healthy relationship with yourself and a healthy relationship with others; when you are able to embody both the vulnerability of being dependent and the strength of being independent, fear will no longer be a dominant force in your life, controlling your every thought and feeling. A life that is not driven by fear is a life that is driven by values like love, peace, and harmony. Jealousy, possessiveness, and the need to control dissipate perceptibly when you take refuge in the infinite well of love that dwells within and all around you.

Fear is said to be the absence of love as darkness is said to be the absence of light. Obviously, when you want to remove darkness, you simply turn on the light. If you want to remove fear, you need to access the light of love within that has always been there. It is as close as the beating of your heart.

Take time to be alone with yourself in ways that don't include reading, writing, or talking. Deep peace will be found in your aloneness, where no one and no thing can affect your equilibrium. Anyone can be alone at any age and in any circumstance, even when there are other people in the room because aloneness is your very nature. Granted, if you have not spent much time alone, without music, television or virtual connections, it may feel scary at first. Practice sitting quietly alone for short periods just observing the dance between light and shadows or perhaps listening to the sounds of nature. Allow yourself to lie quietly in your bed at night relaxing into the stillness as you ride the waves of your own breathing. The fears will evaporate into the light of your own awareness.

The trouble with the rat race is that even if you win, you are still a rat.

Lily Tomlin

Ambition

From the time children begin attending school, they are taught to do their "best" without ever being given a realistic definition of what their "best" should be. Those "at the top of their game" work hard to be their best, and generally believe that their best is just slightly out of reach. Others believe that being their best means being a lot better than they are right now. While such beliefs can create a desire to grow and improve, this very desire to be your best can also create tension in both the body and the mind. Being on an endless treadmill for a long period of time, only to conclude that you still don't quite measure up to your own or someone else's standards, can exhaust the entire system.

More and more people in industrialized societies find themselves in goal-oriented, competitive, externally-focused, and time-conscious cultures. A strong work ethic drives the desire to grow, pursue goals, and sacrifice time and energy in pursuit of material rewards. This generates societies that are collectively caught up in a momentum to do and have more: more stuff, more knowledge, more depth, more experience, more time, and even more years to remain alive. It is easy to get trapped into chasing after bigger and better desires, with the hope that something, someone, or some place will provide an ultimate sense of satisfaction. Each goal reached actually does bring a sense of satisfaction, but it is never permanent.

Many people attempt to avoid their problems by generating excessive work that can distract them from facing personal issues that need to be dealt with. For others, working hard might prove one's loyalty or provide a vehicle for selfless service. For still others, hard work may simply be a creative expression that gives meaning to their lives. Whatever the reasons for putting in inordinately long hours on the job, too much work and not enough play can result in an imbalanced life.

High achievers often have a tendency to over-commit. They pride themselves on their ability to juggle and master many challenging situations that could each be considered a life path in and of itself, like being their best not only at work, but in the way they raise their children, maintain their home, and even stay on top of their finances. Low achievers, on the other hand, often cannot find a meaningful motive to get themselves to take action. Some low achievers suffer from a fear of failing, based in a perception that if they can't do something perfectly, they shouldn't do it at all. This philosophy holds a person hostage to their hope for a better future and sacrifices the quality of their present life. They miss the joy of expressing themselves in their work, their art, and even relationships for fear that they won't do it well enough.

The ego is competitive, judgmental, and achievement-oriented. It can be a wonderful tool to create and enhance a successful career. But not everyone is driven by those qualities and it is useful to acknowledge that life is not necessarily all about work. Take care not to lose sight of just being quiet for the sheer joy of it or doing something creative merely for the fun that the act will bring. There will always be a new goal to achieve before you get to retire. Don't sacrifice so much of your precious time today that you run the risk of experiencing each day of your life as a mere stepping stone to a golden future. Even as you reach to attain your goals, take the time and effort needed to insure that you enjoy each step along the path. Your happiness depends on the joy of each moment, not on the imagined satisfaction that finally reaching your destination might bring.

Self-worth cannot be verified by others. You are worthy because you say it is so. If you depend on others for your value it is other-worth.

Wayne Dyer

Inadequacy

Psychologists say that emotional pain, so intrinsic to the human condition, is based on a feeling of not being enough. That feeling is based on an internal idealized standard that emerged from early life experiences. When children cry and Mommy doesn't come, they assume that this must be because they are unlovable. Perhaps, they deduce, it is unacceptable to feel and express needs. Consequently, many children carry feelings of inadequacy into their adult years, living lives in which they deny their own needs out of a fear of rejection. But the need to be loved and accepted is intrinsic to the human condition. No one ever outgrows such needs.

Ready access to all forms of media can create a propensity to compare one's own life to some of the most ambitious and accomplished people in the world. Such comparisons inevitably result in feelings of inadequacy. If you were living in a small village without access to information about the great accomplishments of people in other villages, you would most likely take pride in being the best cook, carpenter, or even the fastest runner in your community. But no matter how accomplished you are, self-denigration is frequently the fallout of comparing "up." If you compare yourself to the best and the brightest of the global community, your own efforts are bound to seem futile.

Self-image suffers as a result of this feeling of never quite being good enough and becomes a vicious cycle. While just about everyone complains about planning more and accomplishing less, the longer "to do" lists become, the less time there is to enjoy the present. If you work too hard, laugh too little and get up too tired you might be successful at earning a living, but you may decide that it is not the most fulfilling way to live your life!

The next time you find yourself focusing on everything that you have not yet managed to do or acquire, pause to acknowledge all that you have managed to manifest in your life so far. When you focus on what you are and what you have as your blessings, or gifts, feelings of inadequacy transform into feelings of gratitude and even humility. In many ways, you already live an immensely abundant life. If you don't think this is so, immerse yourself in photos or films about people who live in shanty towns across the globe. Sometimes, just stopping to notice can help to lift the veils of misperception that skew clarity.

If one condenses the 5 million years since the emergence of prehistoric man into a cosmic month where 1 second equals 2 years... for 29 days and 22 ½ hours of this 30-day month, little happens. Humans are simply hunter-gatherer nomads. Only in the last 1 ½ hours does farming emerge, bringing with it the development of towns and cities. The last four minutes of the cosmic month represent the time since the Renaissance, and the last 1 ½ minutes reflect the time since the Industrial Revolution. Amazingly, the age of computers, television, rockets and satellites, artificial intelligence, lasers, robotics and biotechnology is represented by the last 15 seconds.

Dr. Joseph N. Pelton

Dehumanization

Instead of questioning the impact that long work hours and exposure to new technologies are having on the psyche of society, our work force is kept running by the liberal dispensation of caffeinated drinks, anti-anxiety medications, and the substitution of mind-numbing television in place of true relaxation. Many people waiver between whether to use their "free time" to strive to get more accomplished or to "veg out" to recover from a hectic schedule.

The invention of the already defunct fax and answering machines, email, cell phones, call-waiting, voicemail, and text messaging create a new responsibility: to communicate responses in a timely manner; that is to say, the sooner the better. The devices themselves are not to blame. However, the more advanced civilization becomes, the more technology

enables human beings to increase efficiency and productivity, the more we are inclined to give up our free time.
Masterminds in the fields of business, psychology, medicine, science, and human potential claim that the hi-tech innovations that afford instant access to the world's storehouse of information, also distort man's perception of time. Human beings may have not yet developed the necessary temperaments to cope with this frenzied pace of life. This is why most time management techniques are no longer relevant or effective. A complete paradigm shift is necessary to cope with the demands of the Information Age.

Techno-stress is the term used to describe the hyperactivity that occurs in the rational part of the mind as a result of an overload of technology-related stimuli. Located in the left hemisphere of the brain, this part of the mind analyzes, calculates, reads, stores and disburses vast quantities of information. Over-stimulation of these faculties dehumanizes people. Symptoms might include a feeling of impatience with any process that takes more than a few seconds and as a belief that more can be done in a shorter period of time than should reasonably be expected. Now, if there are more than two or three cars in a queue at a drive-through bank or a fast food restaurant, those extra minutes of wait time can feel like hours. Frustration and even rage can surface during the simple act of having to wait.

In a time-obsessed society such as ours, leisure has a tendency to fall by the wayside. Precious time and life energy is spent meeting deadlines and attempting to keep up with personal and professional responsibilities. If you have been running on caffeine fumes, suffer from sleep disruption, find it difficult to remember details, or feel too tired to enjoy your life, you probably suffer from the effects of burnout. The prescription requires a solid commitment to put your own well-being ahead of or at least equal to, efficiency and productivity so that you can take pleasure in the more human dimensions of the life experience even as you reap the satisfactions of being industrious.

The state of the world reflects the state of our minds.
Bhagwan Shree Rajneesh

Stress

This is, indeed, the Information Age. It has been said that the amount of data found in just one Sunday edition of a big city newspaper is equivalent to the amount of information that a typical 17th century European acquired over his entire lifetime. So it is no wonder that exhaustion, caused by mental and emotional pressure, is as prevalent as physical fatigue. Over-stimulation of the mental faculties appears to tax the nervous systems of men, women, and children who live in fast paced societies. Although episodes of acute stress have generally been the norm, chronic stress and stress-related maladies are presently reaching epidemic proportions. Work addiction, overeating, depression, anger, escapism, sex, substance abuse, and other destructive ways of acting out emotional distress replace the simple joys of living.

Obtaining cash from a machine and never interacting with a human bank teller, or shopping in a crowded grocery store without ever making eye contact can exacerbate feelings of isolation and loneliness. Social psychologists contend that living in crowded areas can result in so much sensory and cognitive overload that people can't help but withdraw into escapist behaviors. Because attention span is usually shortened when stress is high, cruising the net, channel surfing, or "vegging out" in some other way seems like a perfect way to relax. But if you do not take yourself out for a walk, ensure that you get enough sleep, or consume enough nourishing food and water to keep yourself fueled properly, you may be guilty of self-negligence. If you do not schedule and enjoy "down time," nurture friendships with people who make you laugh, and move your body enough to offset the pressures of daily life, you might want to re-evaluate or re-prioritize your values. When one's focus on survival leaves no space for discovery or celebration, the spirit implodes.

If you have ever been on a downward spiral, you know that it can be difficult to reverse. It would not be useful to overwhelm you with more lists of "to do's" or to shame you for not doing what you know you should and even wish you would do for yourself. Try to ensure, instead, that you do not sacrifice your soul to people and activities that suck you dry. Create your own "down time." Taking just a little span of time to rejuvenate yourself will result in a return of your sense of humor, a first step in supporting joy to flow.

When we let go of the need to be something we cannot be—perfect—we will discover that what we have left is our humanness, our goodness, our belief and trust in ourselves.

Susanna McMahon

Change

If you feel like you are constantly trying to move forward but often find yourself making the same mistakes, then it may be time to challenge the beliefs by which you live. If you are aware of how your buttons get pushed or that you still don't follow through on things you say you want to do then you have a decent chance of reversing the trend. As you bring the causes of your own unhappiness into awareness, you are half way home.

Effort creates tension. Transformation requires a calm willingness to be present and patient with your own idiosyncrasies. Learn to accept life as it comes. When pleasures arise and you feel like you are on top of the world, accept it. And when you dip down into the valley of despair, accept this too. There can be no peaks without valleys. Remain nonjudgmental. New moments will arise and new issues will present themselves. And remember: growth is not necessarily linear! Just because you managed to handle a sticky situation with grace and ease doesn't necessarily mean that you will be able to do that from now on. Each moment and each situation requires alertness. You can build on your strengths but believing that you can finally become free of weaknesses, mistakes, or insecurities would be as ludicrous as believing that you can be free of the need for sleep!

An enlightened life is a conscious life that uses the light of love to dispel the shadows of the personality. Moments of forgetfulness most likely will arise, you may wobble, and you may even fall off the tightrope of awareness. The solution is to get right back up again.

No one can make you feel inferior without your consent.
Eleanor Roosevelt

Suffering

Pain and suffering occur in different parts of the mind. One part simply registers events, while another conjures up opinions about those events. While pain is a given, suffering occurs when pain itself is resisted. Granted, if someone physically harms you, you will endure pain. But when pain is accepted as a part of life, the suffering it evokes abates. When pain is resisted, repressed, pushed away, or judged as "bad," the thoughts and feelings *about* the pain create mental anguish. Even when people are unaware of it, they are actually responsible for much of their own psychological suffering.

Much of human suffering is the consequence of unrealistic expectation. Ideas like "Life should be fair," and "Everyone should be loving and kind to one another," will surely result in emotional distress. Attempts to control aspects of life that are not within your capability, especially the opinions, behaviors, and feelings of others, inevitably will result not only in your own frustration, but in conflict with those who might feel that you are attempting to control them.

You hold the key to your own emancipation. The next time someone says something to hurt your feelings, it is up to you to allow those feelings to hurt you or not. If someone says, "I don't like that color on you," and you interpret that to mean, "I don't like the way you look," or "I don't like you," your interpretation of their statement will cause your feeling of hurt, not the statement itself. Whether the intent of a statement is to hurt you or not, it is within your power to prolong the sting. If you replay the moment over and over in your mind, reliving the hurt repeatedly for days, weeks, months, or even years, you are actively participating in prolonging your own suffering. The only way out is to calm your own mind down by embracing and exonerating your own weaknesses. When you can make peace with your own "neurosis," you will have much more tolerance for the weaknesses and acting out behaviors of others, as well.

Self-Reflection

Identify a painful circumstance that still festers.
Example: My boyfriend ran off with another woman

How have you prolonged the suffering of that circumstance?
Example: I concluded that the reason for this was that I wasn't good enough and then felt insecure for years.

What is the objective truth?
Example: We had been fighting and the other woman was the perfect excuse to force the break-up of a relationship that was already over. I didn't realize that then so I spent years blaming them and shaming myself.

Chapter 3
The Pilgrimage Itself is the Goal

Meditation gave me the faith that there were other techniques of self-exploration than the analysis of my thinking mind.
Mark Epstein, M.D.

Meditation

As a young adult, I read books about meditation that led me to believe that sitting silently would help me become more compassionate, spontaneous, responsible, and calm. These were attributes I desperately wanted and needed to cultivate in myself, so I began to sit quietly for half an hour every afternoon. Although I was unsure of why I felt so much trepidation, it felt unsafe to close my eyes and be alone with myself. I discovered a mind that could not or would not stop thinking, planning, complaining and judging, and a body that would not stop fidgeting. My mind was like a wild horse. I could not reign it in long enough to get more than a few moments of relief from the incessant internal chatter.

I spent countless hours sitting silently with closed eyes, finding it nearly impossible to relax into "being with what is." I felt that I had failed miserably. I was desperate to find relief from the constant commenting, criticizing, remembering, and fantasizing, but could not, despite my best efforts, find a way to quiet it down. In fact, my meditations, which would have looked peaceful to an outside observer, sounded quite loud inside of my head. Instead of feeling peaceful and content, I felt criticized by internal voices that were hell-bent on shaming me for "doing it wrong." But I was vigilant in my quest to become free of the confines of my negative self-image and intuitively felt that meditation could be a way out. I was enchanted by the idea of living consciously, more aware of my thoughts and feelings, but no longer at the mercy of them. But I was losing hope.

Just when I began to feel that meditation was a lost cause, I was given *The Orange Book* written by Bhagwan Shree Rajneesh. Rajneesh recommended that Westerners do more active meditations, rather than use traditional sitting methods, at least in the beginning stages of their practice because, he explained, it is so difficult for Westerners to quiet the activity in their minds. These were the words that dissolved layers of guilt and shame and eventually shaped the course of my life work.

Rajneesh developed active meditations designed to release tension through physical movement and emotional catharsis. I tried each of these active meditations. They changed my life. Unlike regular exercise that releases physical tension, these invigorating and cathartic meditations released not just physical tensions, but years of mental anguish and repressed emotional turmoil, as well. His version of Kundalini meditation, for example, includes fifteen minutes of shaking, with eyes closed, to the accompaniment of drum music, followed by fifteen minutes of free form movement, or dancing, to a more melodic tune, followed by fifteen minutes of lying down. After half an hour of intense shaking and "dancing," I became more aware of the sensations within my own body and could actually witness, from a more objective distance, any thoughts that might arise and fall away again. In the final phase of the meditations, once the movement stopped, I felt lighter and calmer. My mind fell silent and for the first time in my life I understood what it meant to be present.

For minutes, hours, and sometimes even days on end, I had much more access to objective awareness unfettered by the insecurities of the ego. From then on I looked forward to meditating. In fact, I thrived on it. An innate sense of trust began to emerge. As time passed, my heart began to open and I felt more connected to the natural world around me, more affinity with other people, and more intimate with and accepting of my own feelings. I felt nourished in a way I had never felt nourished before.

Meditative awareness became a part of my day-to-day existence. I learned to "ground" myself throughout the day by consciously bringing my awareness to my body and my senses. Whenever I felt uncomfortable or unsafe, an indication that I was identifying too much with my thoughts and feelings, I paused long enough to relax and become more in touch with my senses so that I could return my awareness to the present moment.

Even now, in my private practice, when clients cannot quiet their minds enough to calm their own feelings and fears, I encourage them to practice Osho's active meditations on a regular basis for awhile. Meditation serves as a practice to insure that awareness is enhanced during the normal activities of life. The quality of consciousness that a person brings to an activity can turn almost any activity into a meditative one. Keep your awareness on your senses while you are doing daily chores. Notice the sounds, the textures, the feelings, smells, and colors. Paying attention to your sensory experiences will give the mind something to do so that it can take a reprieve from thinking.

The enlightened beings in the East have never bothered about any psychotherapy. They have not even bothered about psychology or mind itself, because for them the question was not to solve the problems of the mind. For them the question was how to get out of the mind.

Osho

Awareness

Contemplative practices are recognized as an essential element of almost all religions and have been practiced for over 5,000 years. The fundamental belief behind all meditative practice is that divinity can be experienced, or accessed, by quieting the mind.

Meditation is said to lead to a state of profound peace that is obtained through an awareness or observance of the traffic of the mind without identification with it. Mahayana Buddhists refer to this as *citta-matra* or "pure awareness" and the *Upanishads* refer to this state of awareness as "witnessing." With eyes open or closed, when the attention is focused on witnessing the activity of the mind, thoughts pass, desires arise and subside, memories surface and fade, and the incessant activity of the thinking mechanism becomes an observable phenomenon.

Dhyana, the Sanskrit word for meditativeness, translates as awareness of the one who is aware. The method is not designed to provide freedom *of* the mind. The mind is already free to think whatever it chooses. It is designed to provide freedom *from* the mind.

A meditative mind begins to relate to reality as it is, rather than the way it once had believed things "should be." Thoughts can be heard as internal dialogues, perceived as visualizations, or experienced as feeling impressions. The dedicated observer of the contents of the mind becomes dis-identified with the mind itself and ultimately realizes the presence of the awareness that is beyond the activity occurring in the mind. The pervasive consciousness that exists behind the discourse of the mind has been referred to as "the hidden harmony" by Heraclitus, "the Tao" by Lao Tzu and, more contemporarily, the "Ground of Being" by Ken Wilbur.

When we simply remain silent within the moment—without grasping for security, without trying to figure out our problems—all that remains is awareness.

Tarthang Tulku

Practice

Monasticism is the religious practice in which one renounces worldly pursuits to live, work, and worship in monasteries, ashrams, or convents, sometimes located far from human habitation, amidst natural surroundings that provide distance from the values of the "outside world." Contemplative monks traditionally lived in such places of refuge where they could dedicate their entire lives to meditative practices. Obviously, you may not have the inclination to live such a radical lifestyle. Nevertheless, contemplative practices are useful ways to spend some of your time, even if only a few minutes a day.

Nonverbal practices such as meditation, silent prayer, mindfulness, or any other experience that includes astute awareness, are contemplative practices. The silence that ensues as a result of dis-identifying with the contents of the thinking mind is an attribute of those practices. No practice is necessarily contemplative by nature but any activity that results in the quieting of the mind is contemplative, even if it is undertaken amidst the noisy, secular activities of the world, like losing oneself in a creative or artistic project, practicing yoga, swimming, or running long distances with a heightened sense of awareness.

A searcher after truth must withdraw unto himself and keep a wary eye on his old imprisoning biases and beliefs.
Plotinus

Deprogramming

Because the internal dialogue of likes and dislikes, plans and memories, fears and desires operates just below normal conscious awareness, most people are unaware of the incessant chattering that goes on in the mind twenty four hours a day, even during sleep. When a person stops identifying with the part of the mind that collects information, stores data, and creates beliefs, psychological freedom is said to ensue because awareness of the mechanics of the reasoning process changes the focus and intent of the mind. When a person abandons identification with the limitations of time and space, their perception of "self" is recognized for what it actually is: a construct of the mind. Beneath the constructs of the mind is said to be nothingness, no-self, one's divine nature, unadulterated by beliefs and conclusions about who you are and how the world works.

For centuries, meditators have sat observing the stream of thoughts in their minds for the purpose of becoming dis-identified with those thoughts. De-automatizing one's own rational mechanism, as taught by Tibetan Buddhists, for example, is said to de-condition a person from past programming. Tapping into objective awareness is said to provide freedom from the past and freedom from anxieties about the future.

Discovering who you are behind, or underneath the conditioned personality requires scrutiny of your own beliefs and biases. Who are you if not the stories you tell yourself about your past, your family history, and your opinions? Who would you be if you were free of all fear? Behind the personality that has been shaped by your life story, behind the love you received, or the neglect you endured, rests what Zen practitioners call "your original face" and what John Locke referred to as the *tabula rasa* or "blank slate." The *Dhammapada*, a collection of Buddha's teachings begins:

All that we are is the result of what we have thought.
It is founded on our thoughts;

Beyond the thoughts of the mind,
formless, eternal, undefined reality dwells within.

To set up what you like against what you dis-like is the dis-ease of the mind.

Sengsten, Third Zen Patriarch

Monkey Mind

Zen Buddhists use the term "monkey mind" to describe how the mind impatiently jumps from one thought to the next, continuously attempting to resolve feelings of separateness through rationalization about what is good and what is bad. These judgmental and conclusive beliefs unconsciously become a kind of personal hypnosis by which people live. The compulsive thoughts that the mind generates are fear-based in nature. They are considered compulsive because the mind obsesses on the same thoughts over and over again. Even the command, "stop thinking those thoughts," can become a compulsive thought!

When the monkey mind takes charge of your life, worry and anticipation about the future can keep the mind obsessing. If you "live in your head" you may have a tendency to get caught up in the conviction that someday you will be free, but certainly not today. "Someday I will finally be okay. Someday I will be able to get my life in order. Someday, when things change, I will be able to relax and enjoy."

Whether you are a "doer" who can always find an excuse to stay in a manic lifestyle or a depressant who can find reasons to justify a negative outlook or a passive stance on life, obsessive thinking in one direction or the other is generally the cause. As long as the mind is generating its ceaseless tirade of opinions, judgments, and obsessions, you will miss the present moment and the essence that dwells beneath the surface of the thinking mind. Objective awareness will assist you to become more aware of your thoughts without being trapped by them and sensitize you to the wonders of the natural world around you.

If the moon or the stars were only visible one night a year everyone would stop their lives and celebrate the experience. Profound awareness of the fact that you live on a globe that floats in space and that you stay rooted to that orb through a gravitational pull, is the kind of insight that looking at the night skies with fresh eyes can evoke. The monkey mind is a layer of smog that prevents a person from being able to notice the miracles of existence. Awareness releases the soul from the imprisonment of mundane perceptions of the mind that arise as a result of being caught up in the routines of modern living.

It is essential to come to the point where you DECIDE that enough is enough. You decide that the seeking is over.

Osho

Enlightened Living

> Enlightenment is not a destination. It is your natural state of consciousness. It is who you are beyond your story.

Despite the common myths about enlightenment that imply a lofty end goal, it is not a heavenly state that embodies everything that is deemed to be "good," but rather it includes all form and all formlessness contained within one universal consciousness. Enlightenment, then, is a word that describes the inherent consciousness that exists beyond one's story, even as it includes that story. But as a result of the six years of research I did on the subject, I prefer to use the term enlightened living.

Enlightenment is not a destination. It is your natural state of consciousness. It is who you are beyond your story. So enlightened living is an art that involves being more fully in the present even while executing plans for the future and learning from lessons of the past. Being present to the moment dramatically affects the way a person lives and works. While a successful outcome will still require preparation, anxieties related to attaining a specific outcome lose their hold. Like any art, however, it takes time, patience, and perseverance to master.

The mind-identified state is severely dysfunctional. It is a form of insanity. Almost everyone is suffering from this illness in varying degrees. The moment you realize this, there can be no more resentment. How can you resent someone's illness? The only appropriate response is compassion.

Eckhart Tolle

Liberation

Liberation from the cycle of suffering does not mean the death of the personality. On the contrary, liberation requires the acceptance of every aspect of one's personality, every human quality: positive and negative; light and dark. It requires ruthless honesty. To establish the kind of environment in which such honesty can thrive, it is helpful to realize that all feelings have value. Consciousness, like love, is all inclusive. It includes and embraces the full range of human experience. Thoughts are just thoughts. Emotions are just emotions. When the mind judges, when it concludes that something is wrong with either you, someone else, or the world at large, the feeling of being out of control and separate causes personal suffering.

Because it is the nature of the mind to remain oriented toward a future goal, this can create an internal conflict between how you actually are and who you think you should be. Young people will always long to be older, poor people richer, and on and on it goes. The mind's promise that *someday*, once you have enough, once all goals are reached, then, finally, you will be happy, is the myth that makes the world go round. The very willingness to accept "whatever is," regardless of how the mind may label it, is the ultimate liberation.

Chapter 4
Toward a Positive Psychology

If you view all the things that happen to you,
both good and bad, as opportunities,
then you operate out of a higher level of consciousness.
Les Brown

Attitude

Proponents of the psychology of consciousness define normal consciousness as a perception that can be recognized, through sensory experimentation, to be only a representation of a constructed reality. From this perspective, events are, in actuality, neutral. The way a person thinks about an experience is what makes their experience pleasurable or painful. That is why one person feels good about himself while another feels self-loathing. Fortunately, thoughts can be changed. When thoughts are changed, feelings change.

Most people tend to see themselves as victims of their problems, which are caused by circumstances that are outside of their control. It is because so many people have a limited awareness of themselves that they cannot connect cause and effect. Although catching a cold, feeling run down, or even waking up in a foul mood are all natural parts of the human experience, the ego tends to feel victimized when it feels that it is not in control. It can slip into a "poor me" frame of mind. Because it "wants what it wants when it wants it," the ego tends to spiral into a funk when it doesn't get what it wants. This attachment to the belief that life should give you what you want is the cause of much psychological suffering. But no matter how well you conduct your life, there will be times when you get sick and ultimately, like every other living thing, die. But until then, you have a choice as to whether to stumble through life in a fog or to awaken from the dream state into a life where choices are made from a heightened state of awareness.

You can create your own happiness. Although you might be able to make a case that you spend much of your life in pursuit of happiness, it is possible, if you do not believe that you are entitled to it, that you sabotage opportunities that could ultimately make you happy. Remember, the more joy you have, the more you will have to give. Allow your radiance to shine forth. It is there. It has always been there. It may just be buried beneath the rubble of insecurity and unworthiness.

No one ever has it all together.
That is like trying to eat once and for all.
Marilyn Grey

Self-Improvement

American culture is permeated with psychological catch phrases like "working on yourself" that imply that struggle is an implicit aspect of growth. It is not. Positive psychology does not require "work" in the traditional sense of the word; it requires awareness. An open heart and a willingness to acknowledge your own value is the preliminary requirement of waking up. Terms like "working on yourself" and "dealing with your issues" are irrelevant to positive psychology because "efforting," in the traditional sense of the word, does not apply.

Positive psychology does not require "work" in the traditional sense of the word; it requires awareness.

Some people resign themselves to fate and make do with what they have while others try to improve parts of themselves that they dislike. It is natural to have ideas about how you and other people should be and to want to attain that ideal. Even people with high self-esteem enjoy the process of tweaking and adjusting aspects of themselves that may seem to them not up to standard. But in the very effort to become someone better, you may lose sight of who you actually are.

Positive thinking, not to be confused with the model of positive psychology, has gained wide acceptance as a technique for self-improvement. Some people have found it to be quite useful. It has, however, a major drawback. It requires the repression and denial of authentic thoughts and feelings. These thoughts and feelings will lurk in the unconscious, and ultimately find expression, however unwanted, in behavior.

Imagine a person who continuously raises the bar on how she ought to be. She ultimately wants to feel okay about herself; to be free of self-judgment. But each time she attempts to improve herself, the cycle of self-recrimination repeats. When she stops long enough to see that she will never feel at peace with herself because she continuously raises the bar, the struggle will halt, she can relax, and a newfound sense of "making peace with her neurosis" will take the place of her self-loathing. The irony is that growth and change will still occur; not by wanting to change herself but by accepting that where she is is where she is. Out of that acceptance change will naturally occur.

This is not to say that enlightened or conscious living is a lifestyle that is free of problems, fears, or conditioning. Enlightened living is a lifestyle based on heightened awareness of problems, fears and conditioning. This requires a quality of attention that can only occur by means of direct contact with reality. That direct contact occurs when observed reality is neither idealized nor pathologized; but realized for what it is. Only then does one experience a sense of real freedom.

Self-Reflection

What is the belief, or "should," that filters the way you feel about yourself?

Example: I should weigh less.

How would your life be different if you consciously removed that filter?

Example: I would judge myself less, feel more at home in my body, and may even feel more inclined to exercise.

Take your life in your own hands and what happens?
A terrible thing: no one is to blame.
Erica Jong

How Thoughts Affect Feelings

Most people do not think about changing when their life is flowing along and they are feeling good about themselves. The desire to change is often precipitated by painful events. Pain can be an excellent incentive for transforming a life. Change, even from a dysfunctional routine, however, can also bring feelings of vulnerability. It is generally uncomfortable to transcend an old sense of self that requires leaving old routines behind, even when you know you have outgrown them. Indeed, many people who are willing to make changes in their lives truly do not know how. They simply lack the tools.

Behavior change begins with the premise that there are only two things that an individual can actually control: their own attitudes and their own behavior. Although you cannot always control the events that occur in your life, you can control how you think about those events. And the way that you think about them ultimately determines how you feel about them.

It is considered quite normal to blame people and events for the way that you feel. And it is more common than not to hear declarations like, "You make me mad!" or "The bills make me stressed." Ultimately, however, it is the way that you respond to people and experiences, not the people and experiences themselves that determine how they affect you. Obviously, bills are merely inanimate objects, incapable of manipulating human emotion. It is the thoughts and pressures that are attributed to bills that actually cause the stress, not the bills themselves.

If you are going to take responsibility for how feelings and reactions relate to thoughts and beliefs, "You make me mad!" is more accurately stated: "I allow myself to feel angry when you behave that way." When a behavior violates your values, as a result of the ego's resistance to include other points of view, anger arises. If you bring your awareness to the situation, you can choose whether or not to give your power to the person or situation you do not approve of. You do have the option of simply noticing that the differences between you and the other provoke feelings that you do not necessarily have to indulge. Once you understand this to be true, it becomes impossible to attribute personal dissatisfaction solely to someone else's behavior.

Happiness is wanting what you get.
Warren Buffet

Self-Imposed Suffering

When the world does not match your ideal, it causes the mind to worry, withdraw, or participate in the sometimes overwhelming task of trying to change things. But trying to control the uncontrollable can result in unnecessary, self-imposed suffering. For example, if you feel sad when it rains because you prefer sunny days, your preferences dictate your feelings. Wanting to change aspects of people and events that are not within your control is the source of much psychological distress. Wanting aspects of yourself that are not outside of your control to be different, like wishing you had a different skin color or height, borders on self-abuse.

Demoralizing yourself with negative thoughts like, "I'll never be able to take this weight off," or "I'm too lazy to change," will de-motivate your own natural inclination to develop. Imagine telling someone else who feels badly about their weight gain that they are too lazy to change or that they will never be able to take that weight off. It tears down the spirit. Such messages are like self-hypnotic suggestions; they contribute to a negative self-image. With just a little practice, you can reframe the torturous, worrisome, shame-inducing thoughts that stifle your creativity and motivation into calming, reassuring ones.

Self-Reflection

How different would your life be if you developed a calming, internal voice that reassured you?
Example: I would be less needy of reassurance.

How different would you feel if instead of scaring yourself with thoughts of impending doom, you focused your attention on how to be triumphant?
Example: I would attempt to do things that I'm afraid to do like bringing up difficult subjects with loved ones.

We are not just our behavior,
we are the person managing our behavior.
Kenneth Blanchard, Ph.D.

Reversing Robotic Behavior

Without awareness, human beings behave like robots. Early coping strategies often become unconscious, reflexive habits. But that does not mean that those habits define who you are or that they cannot be reversed. With awareness and consistency, new routines can be cultivated. Once you discover that your mind is an inadequate mechanism to run your life, you begin to take some distance from the thought process itself. When a thought comes, you will no longer feel compelled to necessarily obey its command. So when an advertisement for chocolate chip cookies appears while you are reading a magazine, although the mind may automatically conclude that eating such a cookie would be a pleasurable experience, you will not necessarily get up to ravage the kitchen cupboards for something sweet to eat. The more aware you are, the more you will be able to notice the extent to which you are conditioned by thoughts, and hence you have the choice to remain neutral. The awareness allows you time to weigh the thought against your values so that you can determine whether or not you wish to succumb to it. But the less aware you are, the more robotic your response is likely to be.

As you pay close attention to automatic thought reflexes, you will be able to more consciously choose how to spend your time and whether or not to say "yes" or "no" to people and situations that distract you from living in accordance with your values. If you value self-reflection, for instance, but are in the habit of spending most of your time in the company of others who are content to lead superficial lives, then you sabotage the possibility of your own fulfillment. Each time you deny yourself time alone, a moment of self-judgment arises followed by a sense of guilt that lowers your sense of self-worth and results in a sense of self-resentment. The more aware you become of how unconscious patterns and negative beliefs affect your own happiness and well-being, the less prone they will be to hold power over you.

It's not enough to come into the temple and divide your practice from your daily life, and then walk out.
Danan Henry

Self-Mastery

Some of the traditional Asian philosophies treat their bodies as temples, their minds as servants, and their breath as the bridge that allows the spiritual and physical worlds to meet. The purpose of life is to care for one's own body, mind, and spirit so well that they can function at their optimum and be of better service in the world. The ancient traditions of Martial Arts, Tai Chi, Yoga, and even Buddhist meditation are based on the concept that self-discipline is a path of liberation. Eastern philosophies emphasize "daily practice," not only to perfect an art, but also for the personal discipline which results from the practice itself. Any activity that includes focus of the mind and utilization of the physical body, including running, swimming, weight-lifting, knitting, playing an instrument, or painting, can be useful pursuits on the path of self-mastery, if carried out in a conscious manner.

Although self-discipline is commonly perceived as a strict regimen devoid of indulgence, the word discipline actually comes from the word "disciple," which means "learner." To be disciplined actually means to be one who is willing to learn. Most people who are repelled by the idea of restraint and self-control generally hold freedom as a very high value. What they do not realize is that discipline can ultimately be a pathway to freedom. This is one of the paradoxes of life. Discipline helps you to achieve your heart's desires. The discipline of saying "no" to your own unhealthy compulsions will result in deeper freedom because discipline allows you to use your mind in service of your deepest aspirations rather than being at the mercy of its every superficial whim.

It's not hard to make decisions when you know what your values are.
Roy Disney

The Value-Driven Life

Consider how you spend your time each day, each week, each year. Do you generally devote your time and energy to people and activities that you most value or are you in a routine that doesn't necessarily make your heart sing? Do you say you value one thing, but in actuality find that you put your energy into other things? If you value your health, for example, do you take the time to exercise and insure that you eat nourishing food or do you hope that your health will hold up despite the abuse and neglect that you inflict upon your body? Most people agree that their two most precious commodities are time and energy. Do you spend your precious time and energy on work that you enjoy, people you really care about, and activities that truly satisfy you? If not, you are not alone. Millions of Americans are unhappy in their jobs and an inordinate number of people are taking antidepressants, not to mention anti-anxiety and insomnia medications to treat the symptoms of their discontent.

Your willingness to own up to your mistakes, to accept responsibility for the present conditions of your life, and to allow others to have their own opinions about you, can be tremendously liberating. If you are self-conscious about making changes in your life, just remember that whatever others think of you does not necessarily have to be any of your business. As much as you may like to believe that you can control people's opinions about you, you cannot. In fact, attempting to do so is actually a subtle, and sometimes not so subtle, form of manipulation. Practice tolerating other people's differences of opinion. They have a right to their own thoughts and feelings regardless of whether you agree with them or not.

Your choices about how to behave, what to do with your time, and who to spend time interacting with will be most fulfilling when you base those choices on your own core values. Of course, if you are in an intimate relationship or if you are sharing a work or living environment, obviously you will need to take into account the values of others. However, if you thought that a particular career would make you happy and it proved not to be the case, you have a right to change your course. If you considered someone to be a friend but no longer enjoy their company, you have a right to move on if you want to. You have the prerogative to reverse past decisions when they prove to be detrimental to you or your loved ones.

Self-esteem arises out of the self-respect that occurs when you live in integrity. Surround yourself with people who inspire you. Engage in activities that make you feel good about yourself. If you do not know what you value or if you are not sure what you like, then make a list of everything that you don't like. Then look at your list and identify the opposites. The following exercise should help you to pursue your heart's desires.

Self-Reflection

Who don't you want to be?

Who do you want to be?

How don't you want to feel?

How do you want to feel?

What don't you want to think?

What do you want to think?

What don't you want to do?

What do you want to do?

How don't you want to act?

How do you want to act?

What don't you want to have?

What do you want to have?

How don't you want your life to be?

How do you want your life to be?

Who don't you want to interact with?

Who do you want to interact with?

What don't you want to do with your time?

What do you want to do with your time?

A "No" uttered from deepest conviction is better and greater than a "Yes" merely uttered to please, or what is worse, to avoid trouble.
Mahatma Gandhi

Saying "No"

Saying "yes" to a job that you don't like because it seems like too much work to find another, saying "yes" to a routine that cramps your spirit, or saying "yes" to people to whom you really want to say "no" chips away at your self-respect. Many people are afraid to say "no" to others because they are afraid of being rejected, and thus, of being alone. Others are afraid to say "no" because they are so uncomfortable causing pain or discomfort to someone else. They often end up bearing the pain or discomfort themselves, because saying "yes" to others can sometimes cause you to say "no" to your own needs and desires. And while indulgence of one's own needs and desires is not always the highest value, sometimes, especially for people who tend to give so much that they feel depleted or resentful, honoring one's own needs first can be an honorable and healthy decision. Although it may seem like a form of selfishness, once in awhile, in the spirit of self-care, you may need to feel the temporary discomfort of putting yourself first so that you can realize how much better you function when you are rejuvenated.

True intimacy requires honest communication rather than avoidance of confrontations. If you only work at meeting everyone else's needs, you will probably end up feeling resentful because you failed to take care of your own needs. If you allow your energy to leak, attempting to be everything to everyone to the detriment of your own well-being, your giving can result in self-neglect.

> When you allow your authenticity and vulnerability to arise, the phoniness of your personality transforms into the uniqueness of your individuality.

It is honorable to meet the needs of people you love, as long as you don't abuse or neglect your own needs in the process. You may even manage to keep up with your responsibilities to others and still find yourself judged or rejected for taking time to meet your own needs. That person may feel threatened by your freedom or resentful that you do not give all of your time and energy to them. Although learning to say "No" can be uncomfortable for both parties involved, neglecting to honor your own needs is equivalent to saying, "your happiness is more important to me than my own." Saying "Yes" to yourself is a gesture of self-respect.

When you take responsibility for how you live your life, when your commitment to yourself is at least as important as your commitment to others, and when you allow your authenticity and vulnerability to arise, the phoniness of your personality will transform into the beauty and uniqueness of your individuality.

Chapter 5
The Mind in Service of the Heart

Imagine life as a game in which you are juggling five balls
...work, family, health, friends and spirit.
Work is a rubber ball. If you drop it, it will bounce back.
But the other four balls are made of glass.
If you drop one of these, they will never be the same.
Brian Dyson

When "Can't" means "Won't"

You would not expect to be capable of climbing a mountain just because you decided to climb one. Like so many aspirations, such an adventure requires planning, preparation, and practice. It does not only require one huge commitment; it requires dozens of small ones, as well. Many people don't understand why they get so overwhelmed by the idea of doing something new until they realize that each "something new" requires dozens of steps before they will reach their goal.

If you decide to do something as simple as baking cookies, for example, you have to determine which kind to make, insure that you have all the ingredients, possibly go to the store, set the oven, measure each of the ingredients, mix them together, grease the cookie sheet, place each cookie on the sheet, put them in the oven, set the timer, remove the cookies from the oven, allow them to cool, place the cookies in a container, and then wash up. That is fourteen steps to one simple goal. Imagine how many steps it takes to go on a trip to Europe, write a book, or master a new instrument?

The next time you hear yourself say that you can't manage to do something, pause a moment and determine whether you truly cannot do it or whether you choose not to. Be clear that if you don't want to put the time, money or effort into something, it is not necessarily because you cannot; but rather because you choose not to make it a priority. If you really wanted to do it, you would most likely find a way, even if it took a long time to execute the plan.

When you find yourself saying that there is not enough time to do something, the odds are good that you are, in reality, choosing to spend your time in other ways. Unconscious use of the word "can't," prevents the mind from seeking solutions. The statement "I can't" usually means "I don't want to" or "I am not willing to make the time to." Sometimes "I can't" simply means you haven't figured out how to do it yet. Asking yourself how you could learn will reverse the pattern.

> Attempts to override fear using positive affirmations can result in internal conflict.

Sometimes, the choice to spend your time diverting yourself away from what you really want is a strategy that is rooted in fear. Handling the fears and concerns that have compelled you to make excuses in the past can be empowering because the longer you judge yourself for having those fears, the stronger they will take hold. The best way to calm fear is to accept it as a normal, protective feeling that exists to insure your safety. Rather than judging your fears, perceive them for what they were always meant to be: communications from the unconscious.

Attempts to override fear using positive affirmations can result in internal conflict. Although affirmations are immensely popular, they can also backfire. Affirming, for instance, that you are a confident, successful, and happy person when you actually feel afraid, pessimistic and unhappy, creates a split between what you know to be true and what you want to be true. If you like using affirmations start with the truth of your present condition: "I am afraid." Then add a statement to that truth that is accurate and process-oriented like, "Although I am afraid, I am learning to trust my skills more so I can feel the confidence growing."

...as we think, we feel; as we feel, we vibrate; as we vibrate, we attract.

Lynn Grabhorn

The Need for Validation

Whether you were cared for by parents who made you feel loved and therefore worthy and valuable, or whether you were raised by self-centered, unaware, or weak-willed adults who did not have the skills or patience to care for you properly, the truth is that your intrinsic value remains untouched. You do not, in actuality, need to do anything to prove your worth. Like all living beings, you have value simply because you are alive. But if you continue to hurt yourself in ways that others once hurt you and if you tend to ignore your own needs in ways that others once did, you might as well have a neon light scrolling words across your forehead that reads: "Criticize me" because when you identify with your wounds, not only do you filter your perceptions through a lens of pain, but you are prone to attract more pain to you.

Children mimic the tone of voice that their caregivers use as they speak internally to themselves. And because children are not always spoken to with a caring and accepting voice, many adults continue to speak to themselves with a critical tone. Because the need for validation is innate, negative self-talk can cause a person to seek validation from others. The search for validation can be temporarily filled by lovers, parents, friends, teachers, and even communities. But ultimately, validation has to come from within.

If a parent ignored you as a child, you have two choices about how to respond to that hardship now: 1) you can identify with the "wounded child" by holding on to the unconscious conclusion of your childhood, that you must be unlovable; or 2) you can vow to never feel unloved again, and provide for yourself the very qualities of love, attention, and tenderness that parent never gave to you. Becoming a caregiver of your own emotional needs is healing.

People who meet their own needs first move through the world with a strong sense of self-containment and with no hidden agendas based in neediness. If, on the other hand, you neglect your own physical, mental, emotional or even financial needs, where else can you look but outside of yourself to get them met? Many people resort to codependent relationships, expecting that if they take good care of their partner, their partner will, in turn, meet their every need. Instead of projecting your needs outward in the hope that someone else will give you the validation that you have always wanted and needed, identify what it is that you want and become that.

I was once struck by a cartoon that read, "I'm becoming the man I always wanted to marry." Whether you are a man or a woman, becoming your own ideal mate will bring you home to yourself and, as an added "perk," will make you a better partner, as well, because your relationships will be built on mutual love rather than neediness.

Self-trust is the first secret of success.
Ralph Waldo Emerson

The Parent and Child Within

Neuroscientist Paul MacLean identified three distinct parts of the brain: the Reptilian brain, related to survival and physiology, the Mammalian brain, related to time, memory and emotions, and the Neocortex brain, the part of the mind that is related to reasoning and purposeful behavior. But from a strictly psychological, less scientific point of view, personal identity is made up of two parts: the heart and the mind, better known as the ambitious ego. Frequently these parts possess seemingly opposing values and desires. The ego may enjoy routine or discipline while the emotional body thrives on spontaneity and self-indulgence. Creating collaboration between the opposing parts creates a feeling of harmony.

When the fears of the heart are made known to the conscious mind, a healthy, well-functioning parental-like voice can take action to resolve those fears. Likewise, when the ego is in service of the heart, it becomes a useful and efficient life manager that is capable of providing an innate sense of security. When this occurs, the heart trusts the capabilities of the mind to solve problems. Thus, the heart and the mind become partners with shared common values: the ego's value to grow and the heart's value to feel secure.

The voice inside your head that gets you up in the morning and handles the dozens of other responsibilities you attend to every day provides the same kind of internal guidance, or lack thereof, that you received from adult authority figures when you were young. It can fluctuate from being critical of your physical and emotional needs to being supportive and nurturing of them. A critical internal parental voice might say something like, "you should have done a better job," whereas a supportive internal parental voice might say, "You did the best you could under the circumstances."

The heart is often referred to as "a four-year old child" because of its innocence and vulnerabilities. Although the term "heart" usually refers to the emotional body, for the purposes here, it refers to the physical body, as well. The physical and emotional bodies represent the Reptilian and Mammalian brains, related to physical and emotional survival.

Those fortunate enough to have kind and compassionate caregivers are more prone to have had an internal voice that is calm, kind, and helpful, although it certainly is not always the case. Unfortunately, not all parents serve as healthy role models, and as a result, not all children learn how to reassure or motivate themselves, even after they become adults. Those who did not have a reassuring adult in their lives may tend to identify with a more critical voice that echoes the criticisms they grew used to when they were children. In fact, they may even believe that their internal critical voice is necessary because without it they would not be motivated.

Luckily, even the most negative and aggressive internal voices can be re-educated. So when the voice of the parental mind is judgmental or cruel, internal conflict arises. Defense mechanisms arise in the same way that they might if you were being belittled by another person. You might even notice the onset of defiant behaviors in an attempt to sabotage the agenda of the internal critic. If the parental voice says, "Wash the car," the four-year old may respond by watching a movie. Human beings thrive on reassurance and encouragement. So when the internal voice is supportive and nurturing, when the heart trusts the mind to be a caring life manager, a feeling of deep peace and security arises.

If we are all responsible for everything in our lives, then there is no one to blame. Whatever is happening "out there" is only a mirror of our own inner thinking.

Louise Hay

Short Term Pleasure, Long Term Pain

Without the development of conscious thinking and planning skills, a person might tend to make decisions that feel good in the moment, but without particular awareness of the consequences that those momentary decisions might cause. This strategy, based in physical and/or emotional indulgence, provides short term pleasure that can sometimes be followed by months or years of repercussions. A young woman, for instance, who is caught up in her feelings, might decide, in a fit of passion, to have sex without taking precautions. That momentary decision based on her feelings without access to the rational part of her mind which would take into account the long term consequences of having unprotected sex, could have devastating ramifications.

People who are dominated by their emotions sometimes find it difficult to step back and see the big picture. Choices are subsequently made according to what feels comfortable in the moment, without forethought about whether or not those choices will ultimately serve or sabotage their deeper, longer range desires. Compulsions and addictions occur as a result of catering to short term pleasures without taking into account or caring about how those behaviors will affect other dimensions of one's life. The positive intention behind smoking, gambling, overeating, drinking, sexual indulgence, or any chronic behavior, is the same: to feel better. But making decisions about what to do with time and energy based solely on what feels good is akin to inviting a four-year-old child to be in charge of your life.

Four-year-olds tend to be impulsive and don't necessarily have access to the big picture. A small child might enjoy eating an entire bag of candy just because it tastes good. They do not necessarily take into consideration that they might get a stomach ache or a cavity as a result of their indulgence because they don't yet have access to the larger perspective about how that candy might affect their well being over the long run.

If you get so caught up in your feelings that you can't think objectively; if you have a tendency to make impulsive decisions because you forget to take the possible consequences of your actions into consideration, don't fret. The more you practice awareness, the easier it will be to tune in to both your feelings and your values. This creates an environment in which conflicting aspects of the psyche can easily and naturally begin to integrate.

Self-Reflection

How can you better care for your own emotional needs to replace the compulsive behaviors you indulge in now?

Example: I need to stop and feel my feelings. Then, instead of automatically going to the kitchen or turning on the television, I will determine what I really want and need.

If you are becoming a kinder, more intelligent, more compassionate person as a result of what you are doing, I think you are doing something right.

Charles Tart

Internal Dialogues

Most people have internal voices, even if they are unaware of their presence. Not everyone has enough objective distance from their thinking mind, however, to consciously hear those voices. When the mind is particularly noisy, it can even be difficult to tune in to emotional feelings and physical sensations. The voices inside the mind often make statements that are not well thought out or scrutinized because it is primarily a programmed, and therefore, programmable mechanism. Witnessing internal dialogues can be a profound meditation.

Here is an example of how a thought can be scrutinized to determine whether it is an accurate depiction of reality.

Thought	Challenging Question
She doesn't like me.	
	Is that even true? Can I really know that for sure?
Well, I feel uncomfortable around her.	
	That doesn't necessarily mean she doesn't like me. It could mean she has

different values than I do. It could even mean that I don't like her. Or maybe I feel intimidated by her.

Yeah. That's it. I feel intimidated by her.

Learning how to question the thoughts of your own mind is a useful skill. Through simple observation you can not only explore the mental causes of your own feelings but you can also realize that you have the power to release yourself from habitual ways of reacting.

What is most important is to find peace and share it with others.
Thich Nhat Hanh

How to Stop Sabotaging Yourself

When the ego attempts to keep you growing by chasing after dreams, and the heart attempts to keep you safe by creating "comfortable" patterns, tension is bound to arise. The heart is drawn toward security, while the mind is drawn toward growth and expansion. If you pay close attention, you can hear both of these parts expressed in common speech patterns: "Part of me wants to exercise but another part of me doesn't want to get off the couch," or "I planned to do things differently this year but there's a part of me that seems to sabotage my efforts." Your fears do not mean to sabotage you; they attempt to keep you safe and comfortable. Fears are internal communications that there are issues that need to be resolved. Once those issues are handled, fears settle and energy begins to flow again.

When the mind ventures off on its own agenda, disregarding the needs and desires of the heart and the body, self-neglect and even self-abuse can ensue, because the mind is capable of driving the body hard to get what it wants. Sole identification with the mind can be as debilitating as exclusive identification with feelings. The mind, without access to the heart, has a tendency to become mechanical. While it can be an efficient machine it is generally devoid of any real depth when it is disconnected from the human aspects of one's total being. A confident mind that has little connection with the heart can even be cold and callous toward the needs of the body. When the mind is in control, a person might be disciplined, time-oriented, and knowledgeable, but prone to be out of touch with emotions. This can result in an almost robotic response to emotional and physical needs.

You gain strength, courage, and confidence by every experience in which you really stop to look fear in the face... The danger lies in refusing to face the fear, in not daring to come to grips with it.

Eleanor Roosevelt

Handling Fear

Everyone experiences fear but how you relate to it determines whether it will motivate or inhibit you. If you are afraid of public speaking and a voice inside your head says, "I'd rather die than give a speech," an in-depth investigation into how speaking scares you can help you to determine how to resolve those fears. If you are afraid that you might say something on stage that could upset someone in the audience, the fear of judgment will probably prevent you from feeling confident while delivering that speech. When you allow yourself to recognize that there is no way that you can insure that everyone in an audience will agree with everything you say and you make your peace with the fact that all you can do is speak your truth, allowing others to have their own feelings and opinions about you, you will be able to proceed.

Once fears are accepted and addressed, they can serve as helpful messages about what needs to happen in order to feel safe enough to proceed. Allowing the fears to come to the surface of your conscious mind is the first step toward resolving them.

When I decided to go back to graduate school, I kept hearing the same questions over and over again in my mind. "What if I don't like the program?" "What if I'm half way through it, $70,000 in debt, and I discover that I don't want to be a psychologist?" Until I stopped to address these fears, I felt immobilized. I could not get myself to even fill out an entrance application. It never dawned on me that I needed to answer the questions. "If I'm too far in debt to quit, I'll finish the program and use the degree to earn a living in some other way that is more enjoyable." Once my mind could prove to my heart that taking the risk would be safe, I was able to move forward with a sense of trust and ease.

Self-Reflection

Is there something that you have always said that you wanted to do, be, or have that you have never managed to accomplish?

If it's not just a matter of logistics, like having to wait until your kids are grown, are there underlying fears that hold you back from doing, being or having that? If so, what is it, exactly, that scares you?

How might you be able to resolve your concerns so that you can turn that dream into a goal?

Perpetuating one's position, however it may manifest itself—as self-image, ideology, fantasy, whatever—is the essence of the Mind state and the source of all dissatisfaction in life.
Werner Erhard

Resolving Internal Conflicts

The resolution of internal conflicts requires the same formula as the resolution of external ones: work things out without fighting, running away, or going against your values. As is true with any conflict, the solution is in negotiation. All positions must be taken into consideration until a resolution is reached. Generally, each party in conflict wants to get their own needs met. This means that if there are two opposing values at play, both values need to be met before a clear decision can be made.

The concept that weaknesses need to be overcome is a popular theory found within pop psychology and self-help literature. But this concept overlooks the fact that strengths can counterbalance weaknesses. The personality consists of both strong and weak qualities that are capable of peacefully co-existing. Older, dominant water buffaloes protect their maimed and young by ushering them into the center of their herd to provide a protective barrier around the periphery. Similarly, when the more dominant, capable part of the self, the mind, wants to forge ahead and the sensitized emotional body wants to tread slowly into new territory, the mind is best utilized as a guardian of the physical and emotional bodies, to insure that their concerns are reasonably handled before proceeding ahead.

Imagine that you had to make a decision about whether to provide a loan to a financially irresponsible distant relative who contacted you to bail them out of a sticky situation. Because it is human nature to want to withdraw from unpleasant situations, there may be a part of you that feels so uncomfortable with the situation that you are prone to write a check just to alleviate the pressure or discomfort of the situation. But making decisions solely based on whether they are easy or comfortable do not always turn out to be the best decisions for everyone involved in the long term. Such decisions require time for the mind to analyze the situation from numerous perspectives while also allowing the feelings of the heart to weigh in on the matter.

Hypocrisy occurs when you act against your own inner values. Integrity occurs when you honor them. To make a decision about how to handle this dilemma in a way that will allow you to take appropriate action out of your own sense of integrity, an internal negotiation would have to take place of the conflicting feelings and opinions. There might be one voice that says, "Of course I should lend the money," while another part might feel that it is irresponsible to enable the relative or fearful that the money will never be paid back.

Asking yourself "What needs to happen in order for you to make a clear decision," can be immensely helpful. "What would have to happen in order to feel more comfortable giving?" "I want it to be a loan instead of a gift," or "I would be open to giving the money if it were a barter or exchange of some kind." Stay in negotiation until a decision is made that handles the needs of each part.

It's not what happens to you;
it's what you do about it that makes the difference.
W. Mitchell

Self-Negotiation

If you can learn to validate your own fears, you will be able to then handle those fears in a way that feels less threatening. Instead of forcing yourself to do something that you are afraid to do, instead of stepping outside of your comfort zone, you will expand your comfort zone so that you can feel more comfortable doing what may previously have seemed scary.

Journaling, meditating, and even exercising can bring the voices of both the ego and the heart into consciousness. Marathon runners, for example, sometimes report hearing conversations between two parts of themselves: one part that wants to quit and another part that wants to finish the race. Similarly, people who keep journals will either write in the voice of the capable, confident internal parent or the insecure, seemingly powerless emotional body. The first step to hearing the voices of both your heart and your mind is to be quiet enough to become aware of them. This requires self-reflective time.

The way you perceive your own mind and heart may be dualistic and divisive even though, in actuality, they are two aspects of one whole organism. Anyone who has experienced meditative states of consciousness has witnessed the impermanence of the thoughts and feelings that stream through awareness at any given time. But for the purposes of this exercise, I ask you to assume that the ego and the heart coexist, each possessing different characteristics. You may identify with and even prefer one part more than the other.

Fearful Heart	Egoic Mind
Mutable feelings	Running commentary
Present-oriented	Past and Future-oriented
Spontaneous	Ruminator or Planner
Wants safety and validation	Wants purpose & meaning
Immediate short term gratification	Delayed long range gratification

A mind that feels disempowered by the fears of the heart will hold a pessimistic outlook. Fears can keep a person in a rut for years so giving the mind the job of providing for the needs of the heart provides a sense of purpose of meaning. Handling those fears with solutions from the mind can result in a harmonious inner life that expresses itself as initiative. And because the heart often feels isolated and alone, it functions well amidst the attention of the mind because it feels a sense of inner connectedness.

A conscious way to journal includes a dialogue in both voices. The heart expresses its fears and concerns and the mind validates those feelings before addressing ways to handle them.

The Heart expresses its fears and concerns: I don't want to give that talk because I will feel self-conscious.

The Mind validates and handles the fears of the heart: I am aware of how uncomfortable you feel about talking in front of others so I will ensure that you feel safe and comfortable.

Fearful Heart: I don't trust you. You might say something that embarrasses me.

Mind: It makes sense that you wouldn't trust me. I've been judgmental of you for holding me back all my life. But now I realize that until I handle your fears, you have the power to sabotage my dreams and aspirations. We have to work as a team. I am going to confer with you about my plans, and insure that I meet your needs so that you feel safe and protected enough to allow me to move forward in my career.

Fearful Heart: It's true that I haven't liked or trusted you. It feels like you have taken care of everybody else's needs and desire but mine. I resent you for that.

Mind: You are right. I am sorry for neglecting you.

Fearful Heart: Okay, I want to forgive you. But remember, I don't feel comfortable speaking to large groups.

Mind: I know you don't. I'll be sensitive to that. I'll do everything I can to make the experience a pleasant one. I'll be well prepared and confident that if I say anything to embarrass you, I will remedy the situation on the spot.

Self-Reflection

Identify something you feel conflicted about. What is the fear or concern that prevents you from taking action?
Example: I want to travel but I also want to save money.

What can you do to make your desire more comfortable? (Do you need more information? A solid, step-by-step plan? Might it help to slow down and meet your emotional needs?)
Example: I realize that if I stay and save my money, one day, as a reward, I will be able to travel without feelings of conflict.

Chapter 6
UnTherapy: The Conscious Alternative

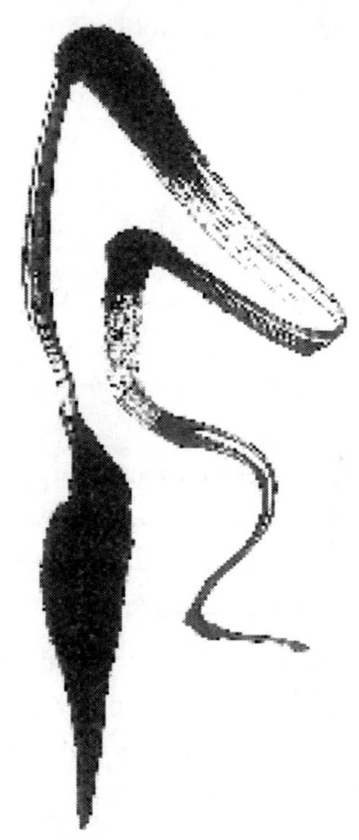

Needless to say, we've all had an oceanful of things we've thought about over and over in repetitious sixteen second segments, all those vibrations of frustration, and tension, and concern over the countless things we didn't want, didn't like, couldn't handle, didn't know what to do with, or thought we had to put up with. Which is why, for most of our lives, we've continued to attract more of the same. Charming!

Lynn Grabhorn

Compassion

If you judge yourself, if you were taught to distrust yourself, if you believe that you don't actually deserve to be happy or loved, if you have somehow lost your own self-respect, or if you do not like how you behave or think or speak, the good news is that you do have the power to change. You strengthened every habit and mindset that you presently possess and you have the power to adapt your thoughts and habits if they no longer serve your needs. You can cultivate envy and anger or you can cultivate love and discipline. It is a question of commitment: do you choose to live consciously or reactively? Although you may feel like a robot caught in unconscious habitual reactions when your buttons get pushed, you can teach yourself to slow down the automatic response mechanism long enough to choose what Buddhists call "right action."

When you feel unloved or unlovable, helpless or cut off, especially from yourself, that is the time to access the compassion of your heart. There is someone who desperately needs your care and kindness. That someone is you.

You are just one of almost seven billion people on this planet, each with their own fears and concerns. If you are capable of feeling compassion for the plights of others, certainly you can learn to feel compassion for your own. If, on the other hand, you already spend an inordinate amount of time catering to your own wants and needs, it may be more effective for you to focus your attention on being of greater service to others. Both are needed: compassion turned inward and compassion turned outward. This book focuses on self-care because so many people, in their attempts to be successful as students, parents, and productive members of society, have fallen into the habit of neglecting their own physical, mental, emotional, and even spiritual needs.

I believe that we are solely responsible for our choices and we have to accept the consequences of every deed, word, and thought throughout our lifetime.

Elisabeth Kubler-Ross

Victim No More

It is not uncommon to hear someone say that the reason for the difficulties in their relationship is because of the way one or both of their parents treated them thirty years ago. An unspoken message that blames parents and the dysfunction of the family is instilled in our culture. But this can be detrimental because it can prevent people from taking full responsibility for their present circumstances.

There is nothing that will sabotage happiness more than perceiving life through a filter of self-pity and victimization. How you relate to your mate or your children, whether or not you can get or stay organized, whether or not you criticize yourself or others, and even how you cope with worry and stress at this phase of your life journey, is *your* responsibility.

> There is nothing that will sabotage your happiness more than perceiving life through a filter of self-pity and victimization.

Struggling is a learned strategy that may have once served you. When you see through all that you have been taught to believe, negative conditionings will begin to dissolve. Instead of defending your conditioned beliefs, determine whether or not those beliefs cause you to suffer unnecessarily. Weigh your present experiences against your values.

You can transcend outdated beliefs, self-images, and behaviors by deprogramming yourself from the conditionings of your past. You are free to recreate your life. The only requirement is that you take responsibility to end the cycle of self-imposed suffering.

The greatest discovery of my generation is that human beings can alter their lives by altering their attitudes of mind.
William James

Using Your Mind for a Change

There may be many explanations for why you doubt and criticize yourself, but there is never a good excuse. You can use the power of your mind to demean yourself, or you can use it to uplift your spirit. Even if it is outside the realm of your personal experience, your mind is capable of being in service of your dreams and values. Once you learn how, the very act of changing your mind can immediately enhance the quality of your daily life because the way you think determines how you feel. And how you feel determines what you will manage to do with your life. So if you do not like the course you are on, challenge your thoughts and beliefs. If you want to grow, you may have to risk the temporary loss of security because as soon as you step out of your comfortable patterns, fears are prone to arise. Fears relating to change often mean that you don't have enough information or that you don't have a clear step-by-step plan of how to even get the information that is necessary to begin.

Whether boredom, dissatisfaction, crisis, or longing for a new experience motivates you to do what you fear, the first step is mental preparation. Painful and stressful experiences like the unexpected ending of a long term relationship or job, can feel like a slap in the face. But such experiences can also serve as motivators to get you to make positive changes in your life.

Sometimes, life circumstances require goals and aspirations to germinate awhile. They may require abandoning the sense of urgency and replace "I want what I want when I want it" with the cultivation of patience. But don't postpone beginning until you are completely comfortable or confident because then you may never begin.

Support and encourage yourself to take risks by providing that extra nudge to expand your comfort zone. If you feel panicky about starting something new, you might consider plotting out small but consistent steps to prevent you from feeling overwhelmed. Any time you come to a step that is beyond your own ability, you will have to add a step for learning. Even in the planning stages, you can step back to gain a broader perspective. Ironically, despite the fears, you will become more comfortable and confident once you begin.

Most people do not want freedom,
because freedom involves responsibility,
and most people are frightened of responsibility.
Sigmund Freud

Perseverance

Not all changes in behavior require research, but sometimes gathering information can kick-start your confidence. A common obstacle during the preparation phase is a lack of skills necessary to insure success. If you want to become a master of marital arts, for instance, but you do not have a clue about how to go about becoming one, you may want to begin by browsing websites and looking at books relating to the subject. People who are immersed in their passion are often quite kind and helpful to newcomers who show interest in their art so don't be embarrassed to ask questions. Learning from someone else's experience can save you time and money, which can sometimes be the path of least resistance.

Aim for mental clarity about what it is that you want and how you plan to get there. If you don't have a plan to get you to where you want to end up, you may never get there. But most importantly, commit to a ritual or routine that will make it easier to implement the steps of your plan. Your consistent daily actions will determine your ultimate destination.

Creating change is analogous to planting a new garden. Once you complete the earth-moving phase and begin the planting and care-taking, the garden will require less time and effort to sustain. But the most important part about making a change is committing to make that change no matter what.

The heart has a tendency to resist change. In an attempt to maintain a sense of security, the heart may attempt to talk you out of new behaviors and cling to old, familiar routines. With consistency, however, the mind can calm the heart and educate it to like and even defend a new routine that it once opposed. Achievement is the result of consistent action. As stated in the ancient Chinese oracle called the *I Ching,* "perseverance furthers."

You grow up the day you have the first real laugh at yourself.

Ethel Barrymore

The Inner Critic

Problems are, in actuality, inventions of the mind. Situations arise and the mind interprets those situations as pleasant or unpleasant according to its projected ideas about how the world should be. Suffering does not arise because of problems. Suffering arises because of aversion and resistance to experiences that are deemed to be "problems." If you pull onto a freeway only to discover unanticipated traffic, the mind might envision a late arrival at your destination. Imagining the unwanted outcome will provoke a stress response followed by more worrisome thoughts unless you can find a way to relax with "what is."

Take a moment to imagine yourself stuck in traffic on a long stretch of road that has no exits and no places to turn around. Even if it's not a situation that would ordinarily push your buttons, let your mind exaggerate the discomforts. Blow the situation completely out of proportion. Construct the worst case scenario you can about how the cars will remain in deadlock for the next 4 hours. You will not be able to eat or even use a restroom. At some point your tale of woe will become so pathetic or absurd that you will have to laugh at the insanity of the mind's ability to perpetuate suffering.

Putting the situation into proper perspective will calm the nerves enough to loosen that grip on the steering wheel. There is nothing one can do to speed up traffic so further resistance will only cause more torment. Consider playing some music or bringing your awareness to the breath. If you are someone who commonly complains that you don't have enough time alone, savor the luxury of having time for yourself. Use such time to relax or to reflect on your life.

Self-Reflection

Identify a person or problem that you criticize mercilessly.

What presupposition do you hold that causes you to have that criticism?

Does that presupposition support your happiness or sabotage it?

How can you change your thinking to insure a more neutral position?

Maturity is achieved when a person postpones immediate pleasures for long-term values.
Joshua L. Liebman

Breaking Bad Habits

In an attempt to keep you safe and comfortable, the ego finds ways to distract you from everything it deems to be painful. It mistakes the pleasures of immediate gratification for the long term joy of authentic happiness. The problem with this is that immediate gratification only brings temporary or fleeting pleasure, whereas authentic happiness provides a deep, abiding feeling of fulfillment, independent of outside circumstances and infused with a lasting sense of satisfaction and wholeness.

Settling for short term gratification is the very root of compulsive and addictive behaviors. The mind experiences a sensation of neediness and concludes that it should fill that need with, well, fill in the blank—food, alcohol, shopping, gambling, sex, games, television, relationships, etc. When chronic smokers enjoy their first cigarette, they unconsciously notice that the smoking provides a feeling that they like. They store that information in their memory banks. At a later time, when they feel a need to adjust their state, the mind provides the memory of how a cigarette once brought them pleasure and concludes that it will bring pleasure once again. The smoker has a positive intention: to regain that desirable state.

Finding ways to comfort yourself when you are feeling "off kilter" is easy; all you have to do is look around for experiences that will make you feel better, even if just for a short time.

Whether it is excessive eating, drinking, drugging, sexing, shopping, texting, reading, watching, or even exercising—any self-indulgence used exclusively as a method to temporarily pacify deeper dissatisfactions, will work to hide the dissatisfactions but not to remedy them in such a manner that they actually go away. When a person feels empty or exhausted, lonely or lost, quick fixes are often sought as a means of providing a momentary lift.

If an overweight woman goes on a food binge to reward herself for a long hard day at the office, afterwards she may feel ashamed for her lack of willpower. Similarly, someone else may handle stress by overspending. Many people get a high when buying something new, but then feel embarrassed about their profligate spending habits. This is why department stores go to great lengths to impart a sense of order. They are impeccably tidy and well-organized. The colors, the temperature, the background music, the lighting are all designed to make a person feel safe and comfortable; an outward reflection of the very state of mind that many shoppers long to feel.

People can spend their entire lives attempting to satisfy internal needs by external stimuli, substances, or experiences that only provide temporary relief. A craving for a sense of self-worth, for example, cannot be permanently satisfied with job status, an impressive car, or a house in a nice neighborhood. Such things are certainly lovely to possess, but unless they are accompanied by an innate sense of value, even the most luxurious lifestyle may only provide momentary reprieve from the universal, primal desire to feel whole.

Habits and compulsions occur when the mind goes "on automatic" without awareness or evaluation. To reverse these types of unconscious behaviors, awareness is required. This is why one of the most successful techniques for gaining control over a habit is to "journal." It has been well established that if you need to gain control of your finances, writing down everything you spend will help to bring unconscious spending habits into awareness. If it is overeating or smoking that you want to gain control over, journaling the details of those indulgences provides a visual log of how feelings correlate to the desire that drives the behavior. Logging details can stimulate insight into the unconscious mind as it attempts to meet internal needs by seeking out superficial remedies that bring immediate relief.

The mind is using you. You have become a slave. The master has become the slave and the slave has become the master.
Osho

Motivation

Many people use self-criticism as a motivation to change. But negative self-talk often sabotages motivation in the long run. If you gained weight as a result of over-indulgence and you don't like what you see in the mirror, you may feel regret, call yourself names or feel victimized by the extra fat around your middle. If a woman makes a New Year's resolution to improve her diet or to insure that she exercises more regularly, but then hears a critical voice inside her head that whines about the changes, it may cause her to give up. But just because she feels nervous or uncomfortable about disrupting her old, familiar habit does not mean she is not ready for change. Many people who feel lost or even phony as they attempt to make changes in their lives have created negative associations about the new behaviors. So if the woman reneged on her resolution, the part that had the idea to take the weight off in the first place becomes the part that berates her for failing. To add insult to injury, feelings of despair about not being able to keep her promise to herself can reduce what little self-respect she has left regarding this issue. This is why some people stop setting goals. They don't want to have to endure the pain of failing or the humiliation of not following through.

UnTherapy provides a framework in which to become conscious of those internal voices, see an unwanted image in the mirror, and feel the discomfort. Embracing the desire to change, when stimulated by a rejection of how you are in the present, is what is actually creating internal conflict. When the weight gain becomes more uncomfortable than changing eating and exercise patterns, this awareness will result in transcendence of old patterns.

Such motivation is not rooted in vanity or self-absorption. True motivation arises out of an objective awareness that allows a person to see the big picture of how the state of their own mental, emotional, and physical health affects not only their own quality of life, but the quality of life of each person who cares for or depends upon their well-being.

The minute you choose to do what you really want to do, it's a different kind of life.

Buckminster Fuller

Focusing on What You Want

The mind is rarely satisfied. Almost nobody believes that they have enough. The fear of not having or being enough drives the belief that more is needed, regardless of how much there is. If someone has a penchant for shopping, they can almost always justify a desire to buy something new. Likewise, if someone has an insatiable appetite to feel connected to their mate, that mate may feel that no matter how much time and attention they give, it is never perceived as enough. In the land of "not enough-ness" the future provides hope for the day when you will finally feel like you are enough, have enough, and do enough. And won't it be wondrous? When that time of your life arrives, you will finally be able to relax and enjoy. Likewise, those who reminisce about their golden pasts might forget or repress the aspects of past eras that were not so golden. Mothers reminisce about how wonderful it was to be pregnant or to have toddlers, forgetting the difficulties that accompanied those joys. Life is always a mixed blessing. There cannot be light without shadows.

The more you can get in touch with and clearly articulate your own wants and needs, the better chance you have to feel at peace with yourself, and thus be able to live and work harmoniously with others. Insure, however, that you articulate your needs in the positive. It is not useful to tell yourself or others what you don't want. It is not a question of being right or wrong, or even good or bad. Speaking in the negative is simply not useful. It inevitably sounds like whining which, more often than not will be met with resistance.

The next time you find yourself in a moment of emotional discomfort, bring full awareness to the feeling. Reflect on what that feeling is attempting to communicate to you. In what way is it trying to bring you back to balance? If you feel like binging on donuts, stop and feel what your unconscious is really trying to communicate to you. Maybe you are physically exhausted and your body knows that sugar will give you a temporary lift. Or maybe you are feeling upset about something and the donuts will help you to stuff down those feelings. Find out what it is that you are upset about. Acknowledge the feelings. Accept them as communications from within. In allowing yourself to be with your feelings, the mind will be better able to address your own needs in an appropriate and effective manner. If you decide that indeed, you want to eat the donuts, go ahead and eat them with a clear conscience. If, however, you realize that what you really need is to take a nap or to have a conversation with the person you are upset with, revert to "right action."

Self-Reflection

Identify a feeling that you get that tells you it's time to do something differently.
Example: I get jealous of someone else's free time.

What attitude or behavior would ensure that you get your needs met?
Example: Adjust my priorities so that I have more free time.

How will you feel while you are making the changes necessary to get what you want?
Example: I will feel less like a slave to my ambition and more like I have a life.

How will your life be different when you ensure that you get what you want?
Example: I may feel conflicted by my work ethic at first, but ultimately, I will feel happier to have more free time.

What needs to happen to your beliefs to insure that you get what you want?
Example: I need to realize that it is healthy to live a more balanced lifestyle.

What needs to happen with your circumstances to insure that you get what you want?
Example: I need to schedule time for myself and my friends into my calendar.

What might you lose while you are going about the tasks of getting what you want?
Example: The feelings of deprivation, jealousy, & self-neglect.

What stops you from getting what you want right now?
Example: I just need to sit down and think this through to figure out how I can remain productive while also having a life.

Chapter 7
Enlightened Living

Love is not something that comes into us from someone else; it is an extension of our own minds, reverberating back to us in what seems to be another person's smile.

Marianne Williamson

Meeting Your Own Needs

When you refuse to settle for temporary fixes that divert you from authentic peace of mind, a treasure within will commence that is infinitely more fulfilling than the fleeting diversions of ego gratification. Simply by turning inward, feelings of fear and inadequacy convert into feelings of safety and security.

It has long been said that the way, the truth, and the light dwell within. Whether you long for love, wealth, validation, security, happiness, or wealth, the source of satisfaction rests in one's ability and willingness to be a co-creator in life. The soul mate you may have searched for all of your life can be discovered in the most unexpected place of all: in your own essence.

> You have
> within you
> an infinite well of
> compassion
> that can dissipate
> resentments,
> help you to
> forgive yourself
> and others,
> and free you from
> feelings of separateness
> and loneliness.

Self-Contract

I hereby commit to taking the following actions so that I can live more consciously and joyously in the present.

The next time I:	**I will:**
Perceive the past through a lens of shame/blame	
Mercilessly judge myself	
Feel like I have no sense of control over time	
Fill my own needs and desires last	
Allow my energy to be depleted	
Give until I am resentful	
Believe that receiving is selfish	
Focus on failures instead of successes	
Show little compassion for myself or others	
Perceive the future through a lens of fear	

Is freedom anything else than the right to live as we wish? Nothing else.

Epictetus

Harnessing Time

Demands on time are really not demands. They are the result of conscious or unconscious choices about what you deem to be important. Some people function well under pressure. Others *think* they function well but don't realize the toll that daily stressors take on their minds and bodies. And still others, like the minimum wage employee scrambling to make ends meet or the single mother juggling more than she can possibly handle, actually do run on fumes. Many people get caught up in the idea that they have to "keep up with the Joneses" and then find themselves hurrying and worrying in an attempt to juggle far too many responsibilities. If you enjoy living in the fast lane, by all means, relish the experience. But if you suffer physically, emotionally, or spiritually as a result of your lifestyle, determine how you most want to feel each and every day of your precious life. Then make decisions about what to do with your time and energy, taking into account whether particular people, events, or circumstances will necessarily support or hinder the way you wish to feel.

Although it is commonly believed that there is less free time available now than in the recent past, surprisingly, the U.S. Bureau of Labor Statistics reports an almost unwavering consistency between "work" time and "non-work" time over those four decades. Although the amount of collective free time may not have changed over the past forty years, the types of activities experienced during that free time have increasingly required rapid attention-shifting and multi-tasking. If you are time-starved, try logging how you spend your time over a seven-day period. You might be amazed to discover how much time you dwindle away on things that are not even particularly important to you.

Regardless of whether you are a high achiever or a low achiever, sensory and mental overload can result in the desire to withdraw. Such withdrawal results in behaviors of escapism, which in turn result in a life that might begin to feel devoid of meaning and purpose. In the 1960's, Martin Heidegger warned that a left brain dominant society, or one that is analytical in nature, would contribute to "man's forgetfulness of being," leaving little room for contemplation or appreciation of the wonders and mysteries of life. To insure that you do not suffer from the "forgetfulness of being," schedule in some quiet time before you fill those precious time slots with items from your "to do" list. Gathering knowledge is a useful pursuit but tapping into one's own inner knowing, unleashing one's own inner wisdom liberates the soul from the confines of mental constructs.

Try not to be a man of success, but a man of value.
Albert Einstein

The Cure for Procrastination

If you procrastinate about something that you say is important to you, you most likely associate some discomfort with that activity. Are you afraid that someone will feel badly if you turn your attention away from them and focus on your own project for awhile? Are you afraid that you might not do it well enough? Or that once you get started, it will be too all-consuming? Or is it that you have painful associations with the actual process of implementing or completing the project? Do you procrastinate because you honestly don't know how to do what you want to do? Or do you only allow yourself to be motivated by the pressure of deadlines?

Are there are a number of things on your "to do" list that you carry over from month to month or year to year? Do you hear yourself saying that you just don't have time to get those things done? It might be worthwhile to look at those items from a new vantage point. Admit to yourself, without shifting shame or blame onto anyone else, why you have not yet made the time to do what you say you wish you would do. If the answer includes elements relating to being too tired, uninspired, or beaten down by the demands of life, how could you make changes in your life, whether slowly or quickly, to insure that you don't ultimately let yourself down? There is nothing sadder than to look back at one's own life with feelings of regret.

To reverse a pattern of procrastination, priorities need to be reorganized. Identify how you want to be remembered when you leave this earth and live in alignment with that conviction. What you focus on shapes your character. Or, said another way, you become what you think about. If you want to be the kind of person who dedicates your life to the evolution of mankind, those values will influence the kinds of work you will be drawn to do and the ways you will choose to spend your valuable time and hard-earned money. If you want to be the kind of person who dedicates your life to family, you will immerse yourself in serving each of your loved ones. Handle each fear that arises so that you can look into your own eyes and feel good about who is peering back at you.

Self-Reflection

If you were to be hit by a truck tomorrow, what would you regret not having done that is still within your power to do?
Example: Take more time to play and to be around people who make me laugh.

How can you re-organize your priorities to live a more balanced life?
Example: By remembering that my happiness is as important as my success.

In the midst of our daily lives, we must find the juice to nourish our creative souls.

Sark

Leisure

The value of life is not in the outcome; the value is in the process. The more you focus on being the best you can be right now, the more each moment is lived well and fully, the better the chances are that the next valued moments will arise with ease. Many career-minded adults say they value one thing, but put their energy into another—until a life-threatening or life-changing experience shakes them out of their unconscious or unhealthy patterns. In a time-obsessed society such as ours, even leisure needs to be scheduled to insure that personal freedom is not sacrificed to a life of too much structure. Focusing on mundane, seemingly endless tasks can result in feelings of overwhelm or anxiety about how to get it all accomplished. Authentic energy arises from the wellspring of inspiration. Exhaustion stifles that source.

It would be unrealistic, not to mention uninspiring, to live without having thoughts or hopes about the future. But many people fear they may never reach their objectives no matter how hard they "work on themselves," how much wealth or status they acquire, or how generous they are toward others. So they drive themselves relentlessly. On the other hand, when the body and mind are relaxed, inspiration and creativity re-emerge. This is why it is crucial that you schedule in ample leisure time. "Down time" is tonic for the soul. The busier you are, the more essential it is that you make it a priority.

Self-Reflection

Identify an area of your life where you "leak," lose, or waste energy.
Example: Too much television and internet surfing.

If you were to arrange your life to live in accordance with your values, what would you do differently?
Example: Call friends and family to show them that I care, invite them to visit, and enjoy getting outside more.

What do you need to adjust to insure that you live that way?
Example: I would have to replace my habit of turning on the TV or computer with choosing instead to pick up the phone, plan events, or get myself outdoors.

Death is not the greatest loss in life.
The greatest loss is what dies inside us while we live.
Norman Cousins

Facing the Fear of Death

Belief in God and in the immortality of the soul notwithstanding, existential *angst* is at the root of much mental and emotional anguish. Questioning and even temporarily abandoning what you think you know about death is a fundamental step to discovering the non-dual nature of reality. The Chinese mystic, Lao-tzu, asserted that to know truth, one must set accumulated knowledge aside and experience first hand the emptiness and insecurity that arise when feelings of fear and aloneness are felt. Across the globe, people attempt to suppress the fear of death and provide themselves with a false sense of security. The fear of scarcity, infirmity, conflict, abandonment, and ultimately, the fear of death have lurked in the subconscious of everyone who has ever lived. Although impermanence is the nature of life on earth, most of us are uncomfortable with this fact. Awareness of one's own mortality can result in an inescapable feeling of insecurity. As long as the threat of change is present, insecurity remains at the core of human experience.

Being exposed to points of view that are different from your own is a powerful way to expand your consciousness. Don't be afraid to put yourself into situations that will challenge your cherished biases. Traveling to foreign lands where beliefs and customs relating to death are distinctly different from your own can provide unique opportunities to become more aware of your own religious and cultural conditionings. In India, I watched in awe, as families carried the corpses of their loved ones on stretchers strewn with flowers through the streets before burning the corpses in open fire pits for all to witness. In Tibet, the corpses are put out for the vultures to consume. Any situation, especially the death of someone you know, can serve as an opportunity to set your own beliefs aside and investigate the nature of life and death with an open heart. Death will come knocking on your door soon enough. The more aware that you can be of this fact, the more you will cherish your life on earth.

Everything we hate, resist, or disown about ourselves takes on a life of its own, undermining our feelings of worthiness.

Debbie Ford

Banishing Artificially Imposed "Shoulds"

Emotional survival strategies, like staying busy to avoid feelings or manipulating others to get your own way, prevent a person from living consciously and responsibly. Bringing unconscious fears and coping strategies into awareness can feel like a huge relief. Those acquired defenses keep the body tense and the mind in unrest. Allowing those defenses to relax opens a person up to their authenticity.

You cannot create the life that you want by rejecting parts of yourself that you deem unacceptable. As you begin to eliminate your need for perfection, you will discover that there is no shame in revealing authentic feelings. As you discover your own value, self-destructive tendencies will drop away. When you value friends and loved ones, you don't abuse them when they share their feelings with you. There is no need to deny any of your own emotions just because they conflict with an idealized self-perception. Operating from a projected ideal about how you, others, and life itself "should be" is the cause of tension. Although you will always have preferences, in the absence of your judgment, everything is just what it is. The words of the serenity prayer provide a healthy and balanced perspective: Grant me the serenity to accept the things I cannot change; the courage to change the things I can; and the wisdom to know the difference.

How many cares one loses when one decides not to be something but to be someone.
Coco Chanel

Wisdom to Live By

My intention in writing this book was never to overwhelm you with more "to do" lists or to shame you for not being where you wish you were. Rather, my intention was to provide you with a reference manual for reversing patterns of self-neglect, a common consequence of the self-improvement approach.

It is okay to be you. Whether you effort or not, you will learn and you will grow. Whether you are a procrastinator or an over-achiever, this book was designed to help you to become more aware of the underlying issues that drive your choices. Learning how to accept yourself as a work in progress and to cultivate self-nurturing will help to develop the internal resources necessary to keep you free from drama.

UnTherapy proposes that peace of mind is the ground from which inspiration and productivity flourish. As you relax into your intrinsic nature, high energy output will naturally emerge out of a profound sense of calm. The mundane, seemingly endless tasks of life that once caused feelings of overwhelm might begin to feel like sacred little rituals. But don't take my word for it. Knowledge without experience cannot transform a life. Let your own light shine and notice what happens. The world cannot afford for you to fall back to sleep. Surround yourself with people who inspire you. Raise the consciousness of humanity one life at a time beginning with your own.

A Final Word

Whether you have read every chapter or just sections of this book that were relevant to your issues, I hope you recognize that despite the "negativities" of your past, you are as "worthy" and valuable now as you were the day you were born. Innate value remains a constant, despite the ruggedness of the journey. A $100 bill is still worth $100 even when it is old and tattered. Every mistake and mishap of your life has served as a step on the path of awareness. Whether you endured destructive criticisms, unmet expectations, lack of support, or false information, you are not broken. Relax into the essence of your being. It is there that you will discover what Jesus called "the peace that passeth all understanding."

References

Ajaya, S. 1983. *Psychotherapy East and West*. Honesdale, PA: Himalayan Institute.

American Psychiatric Association. 2000. *Diagnostic and statistical manual of mental disorders* (4th ed., text revision). Washington DC: Author.

Brand, S. 2000. *The clock of the long now*. New York: Basic Books.

Brown, D. 1986. The stages of meditation in cross-cultural perspective. In K. Wilber, J. Engler, & D. Brown (Eds.), *Transformations of consciousness: Conventional and contemplative perspectives on development.* (pp. 219-284). Boston: Shambhala.

Bucke, R. 1989. *Cosmic consciousness: A study in the evolution of the human mind* New York: Citadel Press. (original work published in 1901)

Caplan, P. 1995. *They say you're crazy: How the world's most powerful psychiatrists decide who's normal.* New York: Perseus.

Caplan, P., and L. Cosgrove. 2004. *Bias in psychiatric diagnosis*. Lanham, MD: Jason Aronson/Rowman & Littlefield.

Csikszentmihalyi, M. 1991. *Flow.* New York: Harper.

Csikszentmihalyi, M. 1997. *Finding flow.* New York: Basic Books.

Csikszentmihalyi, M. 2002. The call of the extreme. In J. Brockman (Ed.), *The next fifty years: A science for the first half of the twenty-first century.* New York: Vintage.

Epstein, M. 2008. *Psychotherapy without the self.* Newhaven, CT: Yale University Press.

Gleick, J. 2000. *Faster: The acceleration of just about everything.* New York: Little, Brown.

Goleman, D. 1977. *Varieties of the meditative experience.* New York: Irvington.

Goleman, D. 1995. *Emotional intelligence.* New York: Bantam.

Hillman, J. and Venura, M. 1992. *We've had a hundred years of psychotherapy and the world's getting worse.* San Francisco: HarperSanFrancisco.

Hora, T. 1979. Beyond self. In J. Wellwood (Ed.), *The meeting of the ways: Explorations in east/west psychology.* (pp. 70-73). New York: Schocken Books.

Huxley, A. 1944. *The perennial philosophy.* New York: Harper & Row.

James, W. 1961. *The varieties of religious experience.* New York: Collier Books. (original work published in 1902)

Jampolsky, G. 1999. *Forgiveness: The greatest healer of all.* Hillsboro, OR: Beyond Words Publishing.

Kabat-Zinn, J. 1994. *Wherever you go, there you are.* New York: Hyperion.

Krishnamurti, J. 1969. *Meditations 1969.* New York: Harper Perennial.

Krishnamurti, J. 1970. *Think on these things.* New York: Harper Perennial. (original work published in 1964)

Krishnamurti, J. 1970. *Freedom from the known.* New York: Harper Perennial. (original work published in 1964)

Levine, M. 2000. *The positive psychology of Buddhism and yoga.* Mahwah, NJ: Erlbaum.

Lind, R. 2000. *The seeking self: The quest for self improvement & the creation of personal suffering.* Grand Rapids, MI: Phanes Press.

Luther, M. 1957. *The bondage of the will.* New Jersey: Fleming H. Revell.

MacLean, P. 1990. *The triune brain in evolution: Role in paleocerebral functions.* New York: Plenium.

Maslow, A. 1970. *Personality and religion.* New York: Harper and Row.

Masten, A. 2001. Ordinary magic: Resilience processes in development. *American Psychologist*, 56, 227-238.

McCullough, M., R. Emmons, and J. Tsang. 2002. The grateful disposition: A conceptual and empirical topography. *Journal of Personality and Social Psychology*, 82, 112-127.

Murphy, G. 1968. *Asian psychology.* New York: Basic Books.

Murphy, M. 1989. *The physical and psychological effects of meditation.* San Rafael, CA: Esalen Institute.

Nadeen, S. 2000. *From seekers to finders: The myth and reality about enlightenment.* Carlsbad, CA: Hay House.

Rajneesh, B. S. 1976. *Meditation: The art of ecstasy.* New York: Harper Row.

Rajneesh, B. S. 1978. *My way, the way of the white clouds.* Poona, India: Rajneesh Foundation.

Rajneesh, B.S. (n.d.a.). *Beyond the frontiers of the mind.* Poona India: Rebel Publishing House.

Rinpoche, S. 1992. *The Tibetan book of living and dying.* San Francisco: Harper Collins.

Seligman, M.E.P. 1994. *What you can change and what you can't.* New York: Knopf.

Seligman, M.E.P. 2006. *Authentic happiness: Using the new positive psychology to realize your potential for lasting fulfillment.* New York: Simon & Schuster.

Seligman, M.E.P. 2007. *Learned optimism: How to change your mind and your life.* New York: Pocket Books. (original published in 1990)

Tolle, E. 2003. *Stillness speaks.* Novato, CA: New World Library.

Tulku, T. 1977. *Gesture of balance: A guide to awareness, self-healing, and meditation.* Berkeley: Dharma Publishing.

Walsh, R. & F. Vaughan. 1993. *Paths beyond ego: The transpersonal vision.* Los Angeles: Jeremy P. Tarcher.

Watts. A. 1957. *The way of Zen.* New York: Pantheon.

Watts, A. 1961. *Psychotherapy East and West.* New York: Random House.

Wilber, K. 1977. *The spectrum of consciousness.* Wheaton, IL: Theosophical Publishing House.

About the Author

Dr. Sunny Massad is the originator of the trademarked system of counseling called *UnTherapy*®. She investigates attitudes and values that promote self-destructiveness, isolation, and self-sabotage and offers an opportunity to be free of the painful patterns that arise as a result of over-identification with the ego. Sunny specializes in issues related to personal and professional integrity, leadership, conflict resolution, and stress.

Sunny runs a successful private practice as a counselor at the Hawaii Wellness Retreat House in the lush Kalihi Valley of Honolulu. She is widely known for the warmth, enthusiasm and humor she brings to her work. She has a reputation for using a solution-oriented, no-nonsense approach to problem-solving that cuts through the "story" to move directly to the root of an issue.

Sunny Massad is the President and Founder of the Hawaii Wellness Institute, a nonprofit training organization in Honolulu, Hawaii, where she teaches an 80-hour practicum in professional peer counseling. This program, sanctioned by the American Counseling Association, contains a curriculum that includes the use of *UnTherapy* to raise the consciousness of each student. Because trained lay people can be highly effective in helping others with similar life experiences, this program does not require academic degrees for entry.

Sunny also has an excellent reputation as a keynote speaker and corporate trainer. She specializes in a unique approach that combines the value of heightened awareness from Eastern philosophies with the practical, researched skills of positive psychology.

Sunny Massad has created two best-selling hypnotherapy CD's: *Peace of Mind* and *Clarity*. She enjoys hearing from people whose lives have been touched by her work.

Sunny Massad, Ph.D.
Hawaii Wellness Institute
3670 Kalihi Street
Honolulu, HI 96819

www.hawaiiwellnessinstitute.org

www.untherapy.com

(808) 848-5544

Continuing the Journey

To find out more about *UnTherapy*®, the alternative conscious counseling process created by Dr. Sunny Massad, visit her website at **www.untherapy.com** where you can:

- learn more about her work as an *UnTherapy* counselor
- book a private *UnTherapy*, hypnotherapy, or telephone session
- sign up to receive inspirational articles from Sunny Massad
- purchase her self-hypnosis CD's: *Clarity and Peace of Mind*
- purchase signed copies of *UnTherapy: A Positive Psychology for Enlightened Living*
- learn how to start an *UnTherapy* support group in your community

To learn more about the Hawaii Wellness Institute, the nonprofit educational organization that was founded by Sunny Massad in 2002, visit **www.hawaiiwellnessinstitute.org** where you can:

- read articles, watch videos, and hear lectures
- join the Hawaii Wellness Institute email list to receive periodic inspirational messages and announcements of upcoming events
- learn about Sunny Massad's counselor certification training and the live web-based distance learning option
- learn about the wellness practitioner entrepreneur program and its distance learning option
- discover how to bring Sunny Massad to your town to teach the counselor and entrepreneur trainings
- hire Sunny Massad to speak to your group

Notes

Notes

LaVergne, TN USA
13 January 2010

169782LV00002B/4/P